THE BEST
LEADERS
DON'T SHOUT

What other leaders are saying about
The Best Leaders Don't Shout.

Once in a decade a business 'How to' book comes along that really breaks the mould, and here it is. Cotterill knows the game and with skill and inside knowledge provides a perfect guide through the pitfalls of management and leadership. *The Best Leaders Don't Shout* nails the course . . . it is a sheer delight. Cotterill has indeed been there and done most of it. His writing is concise and razor sharp and it reads like a novel, a guide book and a mentor to your business ambition. Don't miss out.

Sir Bob Harvey, KNZM QSO
Former Mayor, Waitakere City, New Zealand Author, Professional Director

* * *

This is a very powerful book filled with laser-focused insights on how to lead an organisation to great success. It is one of the few business books I would consider a must read.

John Spence
Top 100 Business Thought Leader, USA

* * *

An excellent handbook that reminds us of the distinction between management and leadership. The former is about sweat; the latter is more about vision, strategy and inspiration. Cotterill laces his prose with memorable aphorisms and intelligent reflections. A very good read for reflective executives and eager students.

Dr. David J. Teece, CNZM
Professor in Global Business and Director of the Institute for Business Innovation, Haas School, University of California Berkeley, USA
Chairman & Principal Executive Officer, Berkeley Research Group, USA

* * *

This book challenges the old adage 'leaders are born not made'. Calling on his wide CEO experience Bruce provides an insightful and practical reference to the key elements of leadership. I would recommend it to any aspiring leader wishing to fast track their skills and career.

Gary Gwynne
Former Partner Colenso Advertising
Founder Rodd & Gunn, Professional Director

Bruce Cotterill has walked the walk and he has now very ably talked the talk. This book clearly identifies that excellence in business is a journey and not a destination. He has cleverly guided the reader down the leadership highway regardless of where they are commencing their trip. Bruce has considerable experience across a broad range of platforms and I found his ideas, examples and guidance insightful and, most importantly, practical. This book is a compelling read and there is something valuable in here for everyone, no matter what your experience or background may be. I am confident that it will provide added clarity and focus to your planning and help you with your leadership journey.

Colonel (Retired) Jim Blackwell, ONZM
Former Commanding Officer of the New Zealand Special Air Service Regiment (NZSAS) CEO of the Kauri Group of Companies

* * *

For over three decades I have observed Bruce transition from successful office solutions salesperson to inspiring Stanford Business School trained CEO, Director and Chairman. In *The Best Leaders Don't Shout* he now shares the lessons, insights and ideas, from his remarkable leadership journey. I thoroughly recommend this book as compelling reading for any leader of business and people.

Rick Ellis
Chief Executive, Chartered Accountants Australia and New Zealand Former CEO Television New Zealand and CEO Te Papa — Museum of New Zealand

* * *

I read a lot of business books and some of them we use as references as we coach executives and professional CEO's to get incrementally better at their leadership craft. This book is one that will be used as a reference. It simplifies and offers practical advice based on Bruce's business experience. Most importantly it reminds all of us leading in a complicated world that leadership is all about the connecting with 'people' and getting things done.

Kendall Langston
Chief Executive, Advisory.Works

THE BEST
LEADERS
DON'T SHOUT

How to engage your people,
manage millennials and
get things done.

BRUCE COTTERILL

*Five time CEO and
creator of 'The 7 Principles of Profit'*

BOOK CLUB MEDIA

Published by Book Club Media

www.brucecotterill.com

Design: Nick Turzynski, redinc. Book Design, www.redinc.co.nz
Cover image: Graffiti Media
Back cover image: Stephen A'Court Photography

A catalogue record for this book is available from the National Library of New Zealand.

Dedication

To Ann and Don Cotterill

The first leaders I ever saw in action.
As our parents, you had so little for many years.
And yet you gave us so much.
You taught us the value of aspiration, a sense of duty,
and what work ethic really meant.
Thank you for a great start in life.

BC

CONTENTS

About the Author

Bruce Cotterill is a five time CEO who took on his first organisational leadership role at just 17, and who describes his career as a "vertical learning curve".

Bruce is a "transformation leader" with extensive experience across a range of industries — notably real estate, media, financial services, technology and retail — and a variety of ownership models, including public companies and private equity.

As a CEO he has led Australian real estate group Colliers, Kerry Packer's ACP Magazines, and iconic New Zealand sportswear company Canterbury International, all of which required transformation, performance improvement and turnaround. In 2008, he was asked by shareholders to step in as CEO of Yellow Pages Group to lead that business through a period of dramatic change, including the restructure of the Company's $1.8 billion of debt.

Bruce attended Otago and Auckland Universities in New Zealand, and Stanford University in the USA, and is a passionate leader of change. A lifetime leader, who focuses on clear objectives, enhanced personnel engagement and improved customer orientation he has continuously delivered vastly improved results through his involvement in organisations.

He is now a professional director with a portfolio comprising six Boards, a highly regarded advisor to business leaders, and is one of Australasia's leading conference keynote speakers.

In his "spare time" he is a husband, father, lifeguard, ageing triathlete, competitive ocean swimmer and frustrated golfer.

Prologue

The best leaders don't shout, but they do communicate.
The best leaders don't stand above their people, but alongside them.
The best leaders don't make waves, but they make ripples throughout
the organisation.

The best leaders don't always talk, but they always listen.
The best leaders don't know everything, but they try to know everyone.

The best leaders don't guess, but they do plan.
The best leaders don't react to every little thing,
but they focus on the important things.
The best leaders don't sit still, but they constantly challenge the status quo.

The best leaders don't hide, but they are visible and accessible.
The best leaders don't carry a burden, but they do carry the culture.

The best leaders don't treat their mistakes as embarrassing errors,
but as enriching lessons.
The best leaders don't know all the answers, but they ask lots of questions.

The best leaders don't humiliate, but they encourage.
The best leaders don't make a noise, but they do make a difference.

The best leaders don't shout.

There is a need for better **leadership** at **all levels** across enterprises of **all shapes and sizes**. CEOs and middle managers, corporates and not-for-profits, self-employed entrepreneurs and career employees. **Everyone can do a better job** of leading and managing their organisation. We need to make **better leadership** a **conversation topic**.

CHAPTER 1

Introduction: It's Time to Start a Conversation About Good Leadership

I spoke at a conference recently. The audience comprised 120 leaders and managers from a range of corporate organisations. 'How many of you have a current business plan?' I asked. Just 20% of my audience raised their hands. 'And how many of you who have a plan believe your people know what those plans are?' Just two hands remained aloft.

We need to give greater attention to the importance of good leadership. Good leadership gives an organisation energy. Good leadership gives the people within the business belief. But good leadership is the exception rather than the rule.

We've all experienced bosses or leaders who aren't up to it. Those people risk failure or underachievement by their team or their business, and they miss opportunities, including the opportunity to help their people to be the best that they can be.

But the problem extends much wider than that. At its most obvious we all experience the impact of poor leadership, which presents itself in the form of a lousy retail customer experience, a fibre cable that takes six months and too many calls to the 'customer service' centre to have installed, or the operators of a new restaurant with a $2 million fit-out who forgot to teach their people to serve the customers.

At the other extreme we see many of our national or local politicians who, based on their actions, clearly have no idea of what constitutes good leadership, role modelling or even communication.

Good leadership gives an
organisation **energy**.

Good leadership gives people within the
business **belief**.

I see it every day in business. Leaders without direction and over-promoted managers without plans. Their people left to guess on a daily basis as to what the best course of action might be. Millennials in their first or second jobs, not understanding what is required of them and unknowing as to whether they are doing a good job or not.

And finally, of course, unsatisfied customers.

There is a need for better leadership at all levels and we need to make it a conversation topic. Something that people can get animated about. Something that people who go to work each day should expect. And something that our various stakeholders, from suppliers to customers, should benefit from.

At the heart of this book is my sincerely held and frequently endorsed personal belief that successful leaders are made, not born. I've written this book to share my 35-plus years of leadership experience with incumbent and aspiring leaders of every size and type of organisation. I've done so because I want to help leaders and managers to be better at what they do. But I also want their followers to be more successful, their people to have more fun at work and to ensure that their customers enjoy outstanding service.

Despite the apparent complexities of our evolving world, the rules and fundamentals of successful leadership are surprisingly simple and straightforward. People everywhere respond positively to thoughtful, consistent, enlightened and transparent leadership. And, successful leaders learn how to identify the right buttons to push so as to generate a positive, fulfilling and profitable response.

✳ ✳ ✳

Who is this book for?

This book is written for people who are passionate about doing a better job. It's also written for those who aren't so passionate but who should be and, with some simple pointers to guide them, could be. It is written for those who find it easy to motivate themselves and love their customers. Equally, I hope the less motivated and customer-focused might turn its pages and find something to spike their interest and enthusiasm for getting more out of life.

From university graduates to potential leaders with little or no formal education, you can learn from my experiences. In short, I would like to think that my leadership story is relevant to everyone who picks it up and finds himself or herself either already aboard or about to embark on their personal leadership journey.

These leadership lessons aren't just for business people. They are equally valid for

This book is for anyone charged with **leading** or **managing a team**. **Small business** people. **Big corporate business** people. And **everyone in between**. Even people running family businesses, associations, foundations, government departments, schools and sporting organisations.

employees of public sector and not-for-profit organisations.

So if you are running a government department, a charitable organisation, a sports club, a hospital or even a sports stadium, there are things on the pages of this book that will help you to be better at what you do.

This is a book about understanding and making the everyday internal and external connections that are central to managing anything successfully. My experience as a leader, manager, CEO, director, consultant and speaker suggests that the advice in these pages is as applicable to the small business owner or operator as it is to the middle manager in a medium to large enterprise. You might be a school principal or trust chairman who is looking for a better way to 'get the messages through'.

Alternatively, you might be trying to run the dysfunctional family business with a pressing need to get everyone onto the same page. A CEO or a senior executive in a multinational operation responsible for managing hundreds of people and constantly satisfying thousands of customers who rely upon him or her to make good decisions every day will equally find something helpful in the pages that follow.

Sadly, many people managing businesses, teams or divisions do a lousy job. The majority don't know just how badly they are doing. Sometimes it's the wrong person in the wrong job. Elsewhere, those who have been around a while get stale and drift away from the important aspects of the role. Many others, however, do an okay job. They make some money, get by and, if you asked them, would say they were happy.

In summary, this is a book for all of you; leaders, managers, division heads, account managers, salespeople, sales managers, marketers, customer service managers, painting contractors, builders, retailers, headmasters, sports team coaches and captains, even accountants and lawyers. It's for everyone who wants to make a better job of their chosen career. In my experience, that's most of us.

Some of you will read this book from the start to the finish, as you would approach any other book. However, I suspect that the majority of you won't. Business books, and management books in particular, can be tough going. I expect that many of you will therefore use this text as a reference tool. Something to dip in and out of as appropriate. You might need a quote for a meeting, an idea to prompt you to do things a different way, or to reference a list of things to do to deal with a specific issue in your business.

You may need a business planning process to guide you through the annual review or a template to keep your action plan on track. Or some ideas to improve communication within your team. Alternatively, you may just want to know the right questions to ask. I would like to think that all of those solutions lie in these pages.

If you want to be more successful; aspire to a promotion and a better income;

What are your **personal goals**?
Do you aspire to **lead a team**?
Are you already leading a team,
but **without the success** or
recognition you crave?
Perhaps you aspire to a **promotion**,
or you want to **go out on your own**?

want to break the corporate shackles and go out on your own; or just head in a different working life direction for a while — then the good news is, you've started already. With this book in hand you can access countless stories of success and failure, learn valuable leadership lessons, identify some of the questions to ask, and tap into lists of things to do and how to do them. All you need to do now is read the book and get on with it.

Leadership isn't rocket science. Practised thoughtfully it can, however, take both leaders and those who work with them on some exciting personal and professional journeys.

* * *

Why me?

So why should you listen to me? It's a very fair question. So let me have a go at answering it for you. This book is based on the invaluable lessons garnered during my own personal leadership journey. I often describe my career as a 'vertical learning curve'. It started when I became the 17-year-old Club Captain of the Omanu Beach Surf Lifesaving Club at Mount Maunganui, New Zealand. It continued after leaving Auckland University and my first real job, selling photocopiers for Xerox Corporation. It picked up pace when I founded, built and subsequently successfully sold my own leading-edge dealership business, the Office Automation Company.

So to Auckland in the immediate aftermath of the 1987 share market crash where I was asked by Doug Hitchcock to lead and revitalise his family business, Realty Brokers, a commercial real estate business, before heading to London via the United States and Stanford University's Senior Executive Program. The UK provided my first global corporate experiences, with two years as Associate Director of REL Consultancy Group. There I worked on transformation programmes with major global corporates such as Compaq Computers, Prudential, Rolls-Royce Aerospace and Smiths Industries.

I still remember being staggered by how dumb big companies can be, something that continues to this day.

A telephone conversation in the middle of the night, with Australian real estate leader Roger Cook, led me to my first CEO roles and rich leadership experiences with real estate giant Colliers Jardine, first as Managing Director of the New Zealand business and subsequently as the Regional Managing Director for Colliers Australia. In the latter, I spent more than 200 days a year travelling from one corporate learning experience to another. I was just 32 years old when I joined Colliers and 38 when

There are **bad experiences**.
But there's no such thing as
bad experience.

I left. Coupled with my Stanford studies and my European consulting ventures, the experience provided me with both the inspiration and depth of leadership understanding that I needed to develop my concept of **The 7 Principles of Profit**, which I'm going to tell you about in these pages.

In 1998 I was asked to help stem the torrent of losses flowing from media mogul Kerry Packer's New Zealand magazine enterprise, Australian Consolidated Press. I did, with the help of a fantastic team of editorial, production and business talent. Over the next five-plus years I learned about the media business and we turned ACP into a highly profitable, if sometimes tricky to manage, business. This experience also gave me the opportunity to observe, at close quarters, the sometimes rambunctious but always canny billionaire. I'll never forget his attention to detail. Equally satisfying was the chance to learn the media business first hand, from my boss and one of the best media operators in the business, John Alexander. He remains, without doubt, the brightest person I've ever worked with.

My career led next to the iconic sportswear company, Canterbury International, where I became its CEO in the mid 2000s. Again, I was charged with 'fixing a broken business', and we were able to change the face of the company for the better and remove the company from the stewardship of its bankers.

But perhaps my toughest assignment and thereby arguably my richest leadership lessons were gathered when, in 2008, I accepted an invitation by shareholders of New Zealand's Yellow Pages Group to become that company's Managing Director and CEO. The company had been the subject of a massive $NZ2.3 billion private equity buyout at the peak of the private equity cycle in 2007. The resultant owners — a joint venture between two international private equity firms — together with their bevy of bankers then watched as the declining industry took its toll on their new and expensive asset.

The Sisyphean-like task called for me to lead the enterprise through a period of dramatic change, including the restructure of its $1.8 billion mountain of debt held by a syndicate of 41 banks. I learned things there about the dark side of the banking industry that changed my attitudes towards lending institutions forever. Ironically, some of those banks are now clients of mine.

There are, I believe, bad experiences in business, but there's no such thing as bad experience. My time at Yellow certainly fell into that category. As former Telecom NZ Chairman Wayne Boyd once told me: 'We all need a few scars, it's how we learn.'

Alongside these challenging operational experiences, I've always maintained a number of not-for-profit and governance roles. From my early days as a surf lifeguard,

There is nothing quite as **complex**

as keeping it **simple**.

Tom Peters
Business consultant
and author

I've always believed in the value of helping out in the not-for-profit arena. So I've chaired a school board and a national sporting organisation. My governance career has included eight years as Chairman of New Zealand's largest home appliances and electronics retailer, Noel Leeming Group, and directorships with a large privately owned property developer and one of Australasia's fastest-growing transport and logistics companies.

Since departing CEO life, I have joined a number of company boards, and led a wide range of consulting projects throughout Australia and New Zealand, for organisations large and small.

The purpose of telling you all this is to demonstrate that I have had, and continue to have, an unusually wide variety of leadership experiences. Each of those experiences has brought it's own unique lessons, and each has made me better at what I do along the way. I can honestly say that I have learned a lot from every role and every group of people I have worked with. These lessons are yours for the sharing in these pages.

After all, what is the point of experience, if you can't pass it on to others?

∗ ∗ ∗

Keeping it simple

One of my main objectives in writing this book was to keep the story simple.

There are more books written and articles published about complex management and leadership theories than just about any other business genre. And while they purportedly offer solutions for today's sophisticated and complex business world, the bottom line is 'leaders today are, by and large, performing poorly', as written by Harvard University's leadership guru, Barbara Kellerman, in her controversial but bestselling 2012 book, The End of Leadership.

Then there is the multi-million-dollar consulting industry, of which I must admit to having been a part. Consulting firms are massive contributors to the complication of business. They do so through the development of their own programmes and frameworks, which are built in-house, and then launched upon unsuspecting clients as the latest business transformation solution. In an attempt to establish points of difference from their competitors in the sector, consulting firms all have their own version of similar consulting products, complete with their own terminology and doublespeak, and of course 200 PowerPoint slides comprising graphs, charts and diagrams to explain it all. As a result, most consultancy offerings are unnecessarily over-complicated. They typically comprise processes that are too long, jargon

Simple stuff works **best**.
It's easier to remember and, most
importantly, **simple messages** are
easier to communicate to your people.

designed to confuse, and an inability to easily recognise what the true needs of the client business might be.

So, there's a confused mass of leadership literature and information out there but there's not much simple stuff. And in my experience, simple is what works best. Simple stuff is what people can get their heads around.

You won't see many business buzzwords in this book. This isn't about Total Quality Management (TQM), Six Sigma, lateral thinking, quality standards, or just in time (JIT) delivery systems. I don't talk about paradigm shift or elevator pitch, knowledge worker or learning organisations. There's undoubtedly a place for McKinsey's 7S theory and Porter's 5 Forces in business literature, but this book is not it.

The simple approach extends to my view of business in general. Simple is not only easier to understand; when it comes to meeting everyday business challenges, simple stuff works best. Simple stuff is easier to remember and, most importantly, it's always easier to communicate to your people. In other words, you can get simple messages across to absolutely everyone.

I've watched boards and executive teams spend one, two or even three days sitting in planning sessions trying to solve their company's woes.

Meanwhile, no one is answering the phones downstairs and the sales team hasn't been consulted about the achievability of their new targets. Similarly, I've seen consulting firms that charge hundreds of thousands or even millions of dollars, appointed to lead a transformation when many of the problems within the organisation are quite straightforward and solvable.

Business, like leadership, doesn't need to be complicated. It's about doing the basics well. Getting back to basics can benefit every enterprise, large and small.

In trying to keep things simple and focus on the basics, I've deliberately made this book easy to read. You can, if you choose, read it from start to finish in less than an hour. Simply scan the messages on almost every left-hand page. These pages contain a phrase, a saying or a key point summary of the detail on the opposite pages.

The left-hand pages are designed to provide something you can turn to at any time. Turn to a page when you need a one-liner to sign off the company newsletter. You might be looking for an idea to base your next management meeting or sales meeting around. Alternatively, you may want some extra motivation to get you or your team through the rest of the day. Treat these pages as an ever-ready and easily accessible resource.

The right-hand pages provide the supporting detail. Here you'll find the discussions, the experiences and the stories that have shaped my view of our business

Ask **good questions** . . .
Seek first to **understand**,
then to be **understood**.

world. They're all original stories. They are either about something I've participated in directly or something I've observed. I like telling stories because stories are what people remember.

In 30 years of public speaking I've never had anyone approach me to ask for more detail about the statistics and theories presented. But to this day, countless people ask me about the outcome of one story or another that I've shared with them. Storytelling works. And that too is what this book is about.

Finally, there are questions. Lots of questions. Questions to make you think, or alternatively to share with your people to make them think. Good leaders ask lots of questions . . . as our mothers used to say, 'Seek first to understand, then to be understood.' You need to get the information before making decisions. The more informed you can be, the more appropriate and accurate the decisions you make and the actions you take. Asking good questions is a critical leadership skill.

You need to **work out** what you
want to **do with your life**.

CHAPTER 2

The Intentional CEO

'What one does is what counts.
Not what one had the intention of doing.'

Pablo Picasso

You may have heard of the 'accidental CEO'. There's even a book with a title that's very similar: *The Education of an Accidental CEO* **by David Novak.**

Well, I was the opposite. The intentional CEO, that's me. From the age of about 17 a CEO is what I wanted to be. The boss. Why? Do I like to be in control? Sometimes, but it depends on the circumstances and the task. What I do remember from a relatively young age is that I like to get the best possible result. Orientation to duty? Absolutely. I always feel a strong need to get involved and do the best that I can on behalf of those I am acting for. Control freak? Possibly. But, simply put, I always liked the impact of helping others to do a good job or get a better outcome.

It wasn't always that way. I was an above-average but not outstanding student. Still, there must have been something there because despite my lack of brilliance, one particular leader appeared to take a special interest in me. Mr Murray. Alastair Murray was our high school principal. He always seemed to have time for me. Or maybe I imagined it. Perhaps he made everyone feel special. But when I met him at a school reunion many years later he had, he confirmed, taken an unusual interest in my career and followed it closely.

There were, despite my youth, several things about Al Murray that I took notice of. I could tell when he was busy, focused or undistracted. There were days when I knew not to say 'Hi' as he strode purposefully through the school grounds. But those days were the minority. More often he was cheerful, chatty and interested. He was connected but he was always the boss.

Most organisations **over-complicate** things. Over-complication leads to **bureaucracy**. Constantly challenge the way you do things and look for ways to simplify the things you do. **Simplify, simplify, simplify**.

He operated at arm's-length. He never got too close, just in case you needed a 'tune-up' sometime in the future. There were a couple of occasions on which I needed such a tune-up. And I got it. Full force. Never to be forgotten. Not to be repeated. Message received. Lesson learned.

He recruited well too. That was the other thing about Tauranga's Otumoetai College in the 1970s. Brilliant staff. Al Murray employed people who were outstanding at their craft but who also connected well with their students. There were, of course, a couple of exceptions. There always are. In our case it was the French teacher who seemed to go out of his way to be a nasty bugger. But exceptions aside, Al Murray put a brilliant team together, one that made a positive impact on many of us.

Unlike most seventies students with long hair, a passion for sports and an indifferent attitude to the more academic aspects of my education, I thoroughly enjoyed my high school years. A major reason for that was the environment created by Al Murray and his team. Aside from my parents, he was the first real leader I saw in action. The things I learned from watching him influenced me forever. By the time I left school I was already leading an organisation — my local surf lifesaving club.

* * *

A lifetime of learning

My business career began in the 1980s.

I started by selling photocopiers for Xerox. I soon decided that I was smarter than Xerox so I left to set up my own business — it was one of New Zealand's first personal computer dealerships. It started with just one person — me! It soon grew to three, 11 and then 25 people in three separate offices selling and servicing photocopiers, fax machines (remember fax machines?) and personal computers around New Zealand's beautiful Bay of Plenty and Coromandel regions.

The deeply rooted experience of starting and running a small business has stayed with me for life. It probably also accounts for the fact that people I've worked with over the years call me a very 'hands-on' leader. I learned to enjoy and appreciate the importance of understanding the detail of any business I've led. I believe in staying close to what's going on and, to be honest, I can't lead any other way.

As a result and despite my subsequent experiences in bigger businesses, the lessons I learned over the years are every bit as relevant for the person running a small family firm as they are to a leader or manager in a large multinational corporate.

Desperate to do well, I talked with and listened to everyone I could find who

You need to work **harder on yourself** than you do **on your job**.

James Rohn

appeared to have achieved some success. I also discovered business biographies — books by successful business people who wrote about how they did it. So, for perhaps the first time in my life I took a genuine interest in reading.

There, in my slowly accumulating library, I discovered the 'gurus' of the day. I surfed the wave of early American motivational speakers who spoke and wrote books about their exploits and discoveries. The writings and audio tapes (remember audio tapes?) of presentations by people like the American expert on the psychology of winning Dr Denis Waitley; the top-selling US salesman, author and motivational speaker Zig Ziglar; and the American entrepreneur, author and motivational speaker James Rohn. Later, the co-author of *In Search of Excellence*, Tom Peters, management expert Peter Drucker, and others also influenced me.

I remember driving across the country to meetings with clients, listening to Zig Ziglar's *Secrets of Closing the Sale* as I went. By the time I arrived at a meeting to sell my prospect copiers, fax machines, computers or perhaps all three, he or she didn't stand a chance. Confronted by my compelling motivation and newfound sales skills, they were never going to escape with a simple 'no'!

Those early books and tapes influenced me in several ways. They impacted the way I went about my business, the way I interacted with my colleagues and my customers and, they reinforced my desire to be successful. Reading books, listening to tapes, and attending seminars added another dimension to my personal capability and skill set. James Rohn said: 'You need to work harder on yourself than you do on your job.' I still believe he was right.

I was such an ardent believer that I introduced others to the wonders of learning from these wizards of the world of motivation. Even my parents became hooked. To this day my mum and dad, aged 79 and 85 respectively, still quote James Rohn.

I was 25 when people started asking me to speak to their team meetings and their sales teams. And I enjoyed it. I then decided that, as my career matured, I would try to help others through my experiences, just as Ziglar, Waitley, Rohn and Peters had done for me.

I've now made more than 1500 speeches about leadership, change, selling, people management, customer experience and profitability. And now, for the first time, I'm writing about my experiences and the lessons I've learned along the way, in the hope that I can spark the interest of others to be better at what they do.

I grew up in an extended family in which we played lots of sport, told jokes, played music — pianos, guitars and even the bagpipes — and danced. My mother was a dance teacher. Everyone in the family, from my grandparents down, loved a sing-a-long. Somewhere in there was bred a comfort with, if not necessarily a desire

Teamwork is fine. But sometimes **decisions** need to be made by an **odd number of people**, and **three's too many!**"

Joe McNally, my former client and founder of Compaq Computer in Europe.

for, performing. Standing up and speaking in public never daunted me the way I know it can many people.

As I said earlier, by the time I was 17 I was club captain of the second of the two local surf lifesaving service clubs in our city. The club up the road enjoyed a high profile. Despite the fact that our club patrolled four times as much coastline, we were often forgotten, particularly when sponsorship funds were handed out. This experience delivered my first real insight into, and understanding of, the power that comes with being a market leader. It highlighted the challenges presented by not being number one in a market. Raising money for our voluntary efforts was, therefore, always hard work.

Week after week, on Tuesday, Wednesday or Thursday nights, we did the rounds of the international service clubs. We visited organisations like Lions, Rotary and the now abandoned Junior Chambers of Commerce (Jaycees), seeking financial support for our equipment needs and building projects. In this environment, out begging for money, I learned the craft of public speaking — how to use humour, to tell a story and, crucially, deliver an ending that leaves the audience wanting more.

I gave, I guess, around 500 free speeches before I was ever paid for one. As the bestselling author and speaker Malcolm Gladwell says in his book *Outliers*, this episode in my life contributed to my '10,000 hours experience'.

And so the learning continued. Desperately trying to prove myself, to myself. Always believing that a problem could be solved or a business rescued. As a result I took on roles that many people wouldn't, often against the advice of headhunters and other career experts, who seemed intent on designing my career.

From an underperforming real estate company, to a magazine publisher losing $1 million per quarter, to a struggling global sportswear business and finally a public equity funded disaster with 41 banks and $1.8 billion in debt. I remember one occasion when, on my eighth day in the job, the CFO walked up to me and advised me that we couldn't meet the payroll that was due in two days' time. Elsewhere, I remember flying to the other side of the world in search of investor funding to keep a business alive. Then there were the unhappy bankers with $1 billion in accumulated losses who treated me, the new guy, as if I was the one who borrowed the money. However, above all else, I still remember the thrill of working with great people and collectively saving hundreds of jobs.

This book draws heavily on the fact that every business I've led, with one exception, was losing money when I took over as CEO and was very profitable when I vacated the chair. The exception was New Zealand's Yellow Pages Group, the former state-owned asset that was sold off by Telecom New Zealand in 2007 to private equity investors

Want to become a **leader**?
Try **volunteering**.
Choose an organisation or a cause
that you can get **passionate about** and
put your **hand up**.
It's a great way to develop **leadership
skills** in a **forgiving environment**, while
adding value to something **worthwhile**.

who saddled it with $1.8 billion in borrowings to fund the purchase. The mammoth interest costs meant Yellow was still losing a small amount of money when I left. Still, we notched up several wins along the way, and drove enormous and positive changes throughout the business. We re-engaged our wonderful team of exceedingly loyal people, completely transformed the customer experience and renegotiated the debt down to $750 million by the time I departed.

Fixing broken businesses. It's pretty tough going, but you learn a lot. In terms of learning experiences, give me a business full of challenges over one running smoothly any day. You don't learn a lot growing the revenue line by 5% per year and adding a new customer every six months. You do learn by challenging the status quo, driving change, improving the responsiveness to customers, and moving your good people to better roles and to places where they can have the greatest impact.

As I've said already, the purpose of this book is to share the experiences, stories and lessons gained from leading businesses in very difficult situations and often in exceedingly complex circumstances. If you're leading a team, managing customer relationships, developing products, making sales, overseeing complex projects or even running a family, I believe there will be something here for you.

Where do you learn about leadership?

People often ask me: 'Where did you learn about leadership?' It's a good question and initially I didn't know quite how to answer it. They still don't really teach leadership in school.

True, some kids get to practise leadership — usually through their involvement in sporting or cultural activities — but even then they're left to work it out for themselves. As a result, some have successful leadership experiences, others less so. The underprepared often fail their early leadership test, which in turn negatively affects their group or team's opportunity for success. This, in turn, impacts the self-esteem of the leader. Some don't get, or take, another chance.

As I've already said, my first real leadership opportunity occurred when, two weeks before my seventeenth birthday, I innocently walked into the Annual General Meeting of my local surf lifesaving club. Then, because no one else was willing to step up, I found myself with the job of Club Captain. Despite my surprise and high level of trepidation, it was the best thing that could have happened to me at that point in my life.

Over the next 15 years I was involved in almost every sector of lifeguarding, including ocean rescue, IRB (inflatable rescue boat) operation, competition (surf sports), instruction and examination, as well as management and administration

There are people out there with **leadership potential** who haven't had the opportunity to lead in a **low-risk environment**. We should **seek out these people** and **invite them to try** stuff.

at the club, district and national levels in New Zealand. By the time I was in my mid-twenties I had become involved in World Life Saving (WLS) and was the first Chairman of their WLS Youth Leader Programme.

Like many volunteers, I was young and thrust into an area of disproportionately high responsibility. Fortunately, I made it work. It also helps to be passionate about your chosen organisation. I learned about the importance of building teams with complementary skills. (A surf rescue patrol needs swimmers, board paddlers, an IRB operator, first-aid skills and a radio communications person.) I also learned to recruit people, to fundraise, to speak in public, purchase equipment, construct an annual plan and oversee the building repairs and maintenance programmes that go with property management. I employed professional lifeguards for the summer season long before I employed people in the corporate world. Managing up and managing down. All proved to be vital skills for the career that followed.

And I was able to spend a lot of time at the beach.

Most importantly, I gathered that experience in an environment that was enormously forgiving. In volunteering, mistakes are tolerated and errors become lessons. People appreciate that volunteers do their best and freely contribute their time.

Retrospectively, I see how fortunate I was. The young people I've seen come through into their adult and business lives with leadership experiences learned in a range of sporting, service and cultural organisations convince me that volunteering is a great way for any individual to develop his or her leadership potential.

There are people with leadership potential who haven't, for one reason or another, had the chance to lead in a 'low-risk' environment. These people can end up waiting 10, 20 or 30 years before landing the leadership opportunity they deserve. For some it is even worse because the opportunity doesn't arise at all! Wasted potential? You bet.

If this situation applies to you, try putting your hand up for a voluntary role within an organisation that you care about. Or if you think it is now too late — which it probably isn't — then try encouraging your kids to volunteer. As I've already said, leaders are made, not born. Anyone can develop his or her leadership skills. Some may need to work at it harder than others, but that applies to everything worthwhile.

Look out for leadership opportunities — at school, university, sports clubs, service groups, drama club, the PTA, wherever. Just get out there and have a go. You probably won't get paid at first, but people will probably be a little more forgiving while you scale the learning curve! The experience will, I believe, make you better at what you do.

* * *

THE ROLE OF THE LEADER

To provide the **direction**,
infrastructure, **tools** and **support**,
to **enable** your people,
to **perform** their **roles**,
to the **best** of their **ability**,
in a manner **consistent**
with the objectives of the organisation.

The role of the leader

The corollary to the question of where I learned about leadership is: what, exactly, is a leader's role?

I had the same problem answering this one. I couldn't, at first, come up with an appropriate response. The more that people asked me, the more I thought about it, and the more I was compelled to develop my own version. My definition has become something of a work in progress over many years. Unfortunately, every time it evolves it gets longer, not shorter. My answer now has four parts and they're all important.

My first attempt to explain the leader's role produced this:

*The role of the leader is to provide people with **direction**, **infrastructure**, **tools** and **support**.*

A year later I added:

*. . . to **enable** them to **perform** their roles properly*

Then finally, I added two more parts:

*. . . to the **best** of their **ability***
*. . . in a manner which is **consistent with the goals** of the organisation.*

So now my definition of the role of the leader goes like this:

The role of the leader is to provide
the direction, infrastructure, tools and support
to enable your people
to perform their roles, to the best of their ability,
in a manner consistent with the objectives of the organisation.

I am aware that this is quite long. However, I can't get it any shorter. Therefore, it might help you if I try to explain the various components in a little more detail.

1. **Direction** means having your people understand what you are trying to achieve. It comprises an overall long-term vision and long-, medium- and short-term goals.

Are you **clear** about what you are
trying to achieve?
(**Hint**: **85%** of organisations **are not**.)

Leaders must be able to present what they are trying to achieve simply, making it easy to communicate to all stakeholders including employees, customers, suppliers, and so on. Clear direction means that your people understand what you are trying to achieve and are in no doubt about their roles. They will understand and know how they are expected to behave in ways that are consistent with the organisation's values, goals and standards.

2. **Infrastructure** refers to the various structures and processes needed to ensure the organisation can operate efficiently and effectively. This includes the definition of key roles, reporting lines, people resources, processes, authority levels, and so on. Good processes ensure that things like order fulfilment, billing, financial management, handling customer enquiries and complaints, and all other aspects of the 'daily grind' are well managed. Well-led enterprises don't have to waste time and energy on this stuff. Infrastructure is all about having the right people in the right roles — be it for a call centre, an outbound sales team, a research unit or whatever. This stuff must be sorted, appropriately resourced and left alone so that the organisation can get on with what it does best.

3. **Tools** are the easy stuff like premises, computers, vehicles, software licences, internet access and so on. Some tools comprise the basic hardware and facilities for the day-to-day business operation. Others might be project specific. Whatever they are, the leaders need to make sure the necessary tools are in place. When they're not, a clear approach or process is needed to deploy them.

4. **Support** comes in many forms. The goal is to ensure that your people can do a great job for the business. Once people know what they're trying to achieve and have the enablers — structures, processes and tools — in place, they need to know that they have the leader's or manager's support. Your people must be part of a management structure that allows them to be part of a team and, most importantly, to understand where they go for leadership and input. A good support structure enables the organisation and all the people within it to effectively manage the various relationships — both internally and externally — across the business. They may need you, the leader, to call a difficult customer or help handle a complaint. If you can't or won't, why should they? A CEO should, from time to time, run the sales meeting. Why? Partly to show that he or she can. But it also shows that the leader is in touch with the sales team's challenges and able to respond with the kind of constructive input and ideas that contribute to the process. Leaders must play many roles including problem solver, communicator, cheerleader, motivator, agitator, rainmaker and co-coordinator . . . the list goes on. Give people the support they need to enable them to do a good job for everyone.

The **vast majority** of people **go to work** every day and try to do the **best that they can**.
When that **isn't good enough**, it might be **you** who's **failing** rather than **them**.

5. Enabling people to perform their roles *'to the best of their ability'* is pretty self-explanatory, once they have the knowledge and support around them to enable them to be the best they can be.

6. My final extension, *'in a manner that is **consistent with the goals** of the organisation'*, is all about getting people working on the stuff that is critical to achieving the enterprise's goals. Most people go to their jobs every day and have to guess as to what might be important. As the leader you need your team to come to work and focus on the critical stuff that makes a difference and contributes to the direction you are pursuing. Your people will get excited about contributing when they are doing more than just 'filling a seat'.

Items 1–4 above provide people with knowledge about the company's aspirations and expectations and the tools to do a good job. I always believe that people want to come to work each day and do a good job. In order to do that they need to be enabled with all the tools, knowledge and support that you can give them. In my experience they'll contribute well beyond your expectations if they're engaged, made to feel important, feel that they are listened to and believe they can make a contribution. These things happen when people know what's going on.

To go back to the top of the definition, the key here is to be clear about the objectives of the organisation and to make sure that your people know what those objectives are and how their role plays a part in accomplishing them.

* * *

The things we can control

We live in a world full of distractions. There are plenty of things going on out there that affect our businesses. In some cases they have a direct influence on our ability to be successful. Think about it:

- exchange rates can affect our cost of buying and the margins we make when we sell;
- commodity prices can impact the business of those of us who need to transport goods or supply services to clients who deal in such commodities;
- political stability, or even the perception thereof, can influence market confidence and hence impact sales;
- financial markets have proven to be able to bring entire economies to their knees, often in unforeseen ways.

Be careful to **focus your efforts** on the things that you **can influence** — the things that you **can control**. Focusing on anything else is a **waste of effort and time**.

In recent years we have seen most of the world's major commodities such as oil, iron ore, coal and even milk powder collapse to previously unimagined levels. We've seen major economies such as Greece, and to a lesser extent Spain and Italy, fail. An enormous influx of refugees from the Middle East has raided Europe's borders, resulting in uncertainty with global economic and geopolitical ramifications.

And it doesn't stop there. Britain's public have voted to leave the European Union, with short- and long-term consequences for both sides. The USA electorate has broken with tradition to vote a businessman, and a controversial one at that, rather than a politician, to become their President. And most recently, we have seen the voters of France send a strong message to the political establishment, by overlooking the traditional parties of government and electing Emmanuel Macron as their new President.

All of these happenings affect market confidence and the performance of the business environment that we all operate in. They create uncertainty. They contribute to negative debate, which in turn influences the attitudes of the people we deal with every day. I often see people rolling out the list of excuses for their poor performance. These things regularly surface. They are usually accompanied by complaints about traffic, government, taxes, and sometimes even the weather.

Here's the point. None of us can do anything about this stuff. Sure it affects us. It affects our business. It affects markets. It affects our cost of goods or our customers' preferences. I have seen a business recently that is at risk of failing, primarily because of the exchange rate.

BUT . . . there is nothing that we — you and I — can do about it.

In other words, there are, and always will be, a number of things going on out there that are out of our control and yet impact our business. The first question to ask is, Can I do anything about that? If not, move on.

Instead we should be focusing on the things we can control. Even in the most inhospitable of environments, if we do the very best that we can to manage the things that we can influence, we have a chance of being successful.

So what are the things we can control? How do I get started? And how do I deal with the changes going on around me?

* * *

Management is about **persuading people** to do things they **do not want to do**, while **leadership** is about **inspiring people** to do things they **never thought they could**.

Steve Jobs
Founder, Apple Computer

CHAPTER 3

Leading —
The 7 Principles of Profit

'If words of command are not clear and distinct, if orders are not thoroughly understood, the general is to blame.'

Sun Tzu
The Art of War

The 7 Principles of Profit

'I will never return to corporate life,' I declared when I retired from the corporate world for the first time in the late 1990s. I'd just completed my stint as CEO of the combined Australian and New Zealand arms of the global real estate group, Colliers Jardine.

We had a great run during my time with the global real estate group. We returned the New Zealand and Australian businesses to profitability despite a prevailing difficult property environment. Once I stepped down, I received a number of approaches from real estate services groups in the Asia-Pacific region asking me to speak at their various conferences, or participate at their planning sessions and after-dinner events.

With my 500-speech apprenticeship behind me, I started getting paid to speak and present at such gatherings. Turning professional, so to speak, seemed to demand that I develop some good-quality presentation material. My audiences wanted to know what we'd done to deliver our various turnarounds. Most of the lessons were in my head somewhere. Very few of my experiences existed as a formally structured series of thoughts suitable for recounting.

I sat down in my study one day to develop a theme for my presentations. I was

THE 7 PRINCIPLES OF PROFIT

1. Dealing with change

2. Leadership

3. The back office — finance and administration

4. Products and services

5. Sales and marketing

6. People

7. Customers

due to speak for 90 minutes at a real estate industry conference in two weeks' time. 'How will I fill ninety minutes?' I wondered. I began by listing all the things I'd done as a business manager. I tallied everything from running a surf lifesaving club, selling Xerox copiers, through building my own computer and office equipment dealership to studying at Stanford University. I listed the various issues and outcomes from my UK consultancy adventure and my Colliers experiences, running a multinational multi-million-dollar real estate organisation that was coming off what was then one of the worst real estate recessions since the 1930s.

I devoted one line of my yellow pad for each 'thing'. In no particular order, the list included:

- Organise patrol captains and roster
- Raise money for new inflatable rescue craft
- Negotiate a major leasing fee
- Systems review and decision
- Travel to Adelaide to attend management meeting
- Lead property management presentation
- Give a speech to new recruits
- Renegotiate bank credit limits and interest margins
- Attend employment disciplinary matter in Melbourne
- Restructure divisions and decrease head-count
- Replace underperforming state manager
- Rescue a lost photocopier sale
  . . . and so on.

Two days of thinking produced 30 items per page and 20 pages of assorted experiences. I threw my pile of pages into a desk drawer for a couple of days and pondered what I would do with my new list. Two days later I pulled the assorted papers from their resting place and began putting my thoughts into some form of logical order. Moving down the margin, I started categorising the list into headings. It may have been a banking matter, a brand matter, an employment issue or a sales opportunity. I analysed the points and refined the definitions in the margins. My first cut produced 20 or so headings. Too many, I thought. I re-categorised a couple of times. It took two days to complete the list but then, after some creative thinking, everything on those 20 pages fitted under just seven headings. The list read like this:

A **list** like this **provides boxes** to **put your ideas in**, a **framework** for your **thinking** and a **format** for you to **communicate to others.** It gives you a series of headings to consider.

1. Dealing with change
2. Leadership
3. The back office — finance and administration
4. Products and services
5. Sales and marketing
6. People
7. Customers

It was my 'Eureka!' moment. I've had others since, but none quite so profound or lasting.

I've now delivered another 1000-plus business presentations, completed three further major turnarounds as a CEO (I know, I said I would never return to corporate life), sat on several boards of directors, and consulted extensively across a range of businesses and industries since the list was completed. The boards have included a major retail group, a private equity firm, a transport and logistics group, a global franchise network, and a telecommunications company. I've also chaired a private school board and a national sporting association — not to mention another 500 or so Monday morning team meetings. And after all those experiences I haven't found anything in what I've done since that list was developed that doesn't fit within one of my seven headings.

I'm therefore firmly convinced that everything we do in business fits somewhere under one of these headings. Most importantly, these headings represent **the things we can control**.

Much of my career has been spent working in businesses that have had to deal with poor profitability, delinquent personnel, difficult cultures or challenging business environments. I think I've done my share of turnarounds and recoveries. This list is, I believe, as complete as it comes when discussing profit improvement and organisational performance. That's why I call it 'The 7 Principles of Profit'.

A list like this gives you structure. It provides boxes to put your ideas in. It presents a framework for your thinking and a format for you to communicate to others. Most importantly, it gives you a series of headings to consider as you develop a plan for your business. I have listed below a summary of headings in a business recovery plan for a media company specialising in print media and seeking to grow its online business. We presented the list and aspects of the plan that went with it to a print media industry audience in Europe in 2011. The nine key headings in the business plan are as follows (note the words in brackets):

"

How do I get
started?

- Defend and grow core print revenues (Product and sales)
- Aggressively grow new media/digital revenues (Product)
- Become content rich (Product)
- Optimise sales organisation (Sales)
- Attract, develop and retain great people (People)
- Provide an outstanding customer experience (Customers)
- Re-enable our business systems (Back office)
- Brand reposition and leadership (Marketing)
- Meet our financial obligations (Finance and back office)

You might have noticed that only Leadership and Change are missing from the list of '7 Principles' headings. Both are implied in what this list is about. The change, or transformation component of the exercise, was about repositioning an old-style media industry for an increasingly digital future. Leadership is implied in the need to drive the change. We were able to use the '7 Principles' as a format for the development of the key strategic planks for this particular industry.

Being able to structure your thoughts and ideas around clear headings will help you to identify what's important, while staying focused on the things you can control. The 7 Principles offer you some key headings against which to question the performance of the business and identify areas of opportunity for improvement.

* * *

Getting started — your first 30 days

Right now, either you are well entrenched in your current role or you might be in the early stages of a new one. You may even be about to start in a new position. Either way, you might be considering what to do next, particularly if you are considering making some changes. While the comments that follow are specifically targeted at the newly appointed manager, the process to go through is entirely relevant to those of you in an existing post who might be seeking to revitalise the business or your team within it. Even if you are getting a bit stale in your role, try giving yourself a fresh start.

I often get contacted by people going into new leadership or management roles for the first time. Normally the conversation starts with the following question:

'How do I get started?'

How you tackle the first 30 to 90 days of your appointment will set the tone for your stewardship of your new team. If you do a good job of the first 30 days, you

Your approach to the first **30 to 90 days** in your **new role** will **set the tone** for your **stewardship** of your new team. If you **hit the ground running** in the first **30 days**, you have a good chance of **achieving** the **goals** and **aspirations** you have set for yourself in the role.

have a chance of being successful in your new role. But if you get the first 30 days wrong, you are making it harder for yourself, and the risk of failure increases.

As the old saying goes, you only get one chance to make a first impression. And as shallow as that seems, that is what your first 30 to 90 days are all about: making the right impression on your people, customers, bosses and suppliers.

Knowing how to get started in a new leadership role is a common problem.

It doesn't matter whether you're the new CEO, a divisional leader further down the ladder, or a new branch manager in the local insurance or real estate office — kicking off correctly is important. You will, as part of the recruitment and interview process, have heard the views of your intended boss or, in the case of the top job, the board to whom you will be accountable. They will have expressed their opinions about what's right, what's wrong, and what needs to be done should you get the job.

Once the job is yours, the pressure will come from every corner imaginable. Everyone wants to see what you're going to bring to the role. Some will expect rapid changes. Those higher up the hierarchy will soon start champing at the bit for a business plan, change strategy, progress report and some early results. They'll expect you to address the problems they see, irrespective of whether they are indeed the problems you see. Those you lead will be watching for quite different reasons. They will be asking themselves: 'How is this appointment going to affect me?'

All that expectation will, understandably, tempt you to start doing stuff, changing things and picking low-hanging fruit. You might even feel pressured to take a couple of high-profile scalps, in the form of underperforming products, branches, divisions or people.

Tip number one. Slow down. Believe me, you have plenty of time to deal with those issues. It might not feel like you do, but you have to back yourself and form your own opinions. So, before you start taking action, get to grips with what you've inherited. Take the time to form your own views about what's good and what's not.

Revert, for a moment, to the interview processes. Your new bosses have their views of what's working well and what's not. But remember, they appointed you to this role because you're good at what you do. So do it.

Get out into the business and understand what you have taken on. You can look at spreadsheets and management reports any time, and besides, in your first month or so, you can do that in the evenings. Spend your first few days 'wandering around' your new environment. Have one-on-one discussions with the people who now report directly to you and, perhaps, a couple in the hierarchy to whom you report. If it works for you, use the 7 Principles headings as a structure around which to seek out people and ask questions. In other words, speak to people about the back office,

Tip #1:

Slow down.

your products, sales, your team and customers. Find out what they think about the state of the business or division. Ask simple questions like:

- What are we doing well?
- What are we doing poorly?
- Who are our best people?
- Do we have any people who are struggling?
- Who is our most challenging customer?
- Are we at risk of losing any important customers?

'Simple stuff,' I hear you say. Absolutely. But remember, you're only trying to get a feel for the current state of play. Because you're asking simple questions and listening for answers, you are also starting to build a rapport with your new team. You are totally engaged and genuinely interested in what your people have to say.

It may not look like it at the time but you're also starting to develop a view of your team members. Look out for the signs. You'll see people genuinely doing their best. They might be a bit cautious about sharing their views but, when they do, it will in all likelihood be meaningful and accurate.

Then you'll get the blowhards. This is their opportunity to impress the new boss, and they are not going to let that opportunity go without you getting their opinions. They stand out early, give you their opinion on everything, most of which isn't much use. You'll also stumble across a few duds, people who don't know or haven't really thought about the answers to your simple questions. They will try to bluff their way through, telling you what they think you want to hear.

Now you are starting to get a feel for the business.

Once you've spent some time with your immediate team, go out and have some casual chats with their team members — those who report to the people who report to you. This can be done in a several ways, but keep it low key and casual.

Try wandering through the open plan and talking to people at their workstations. Introduce yourself, even though they probably know who you are, and find out who they are and what they do. Refer to the family photos on their desks and be genuinely interested in them and their families. After you leave their desk, they will tell 10 of their colleagues that you're okay.

Before you leave, ask them some simple questions too. Depending on the size of the organisation, these people are likely to be closer to the customer than you or your team of direct reports, so ask them about the simple things that the business fails to do well. Are there things that they see every day that you might not see from

Try to **understand the business**,
the **people**,
the **customers**,
what you are **doing well**,
and where you are **failing**.

where you sit? If they have a direct relationship with customers, ask them what their customer contacts think of your business and where, in their opinion, any problems seem to be.

Also set up a few group discussions with people. Don't have any more than eight people in any group. Research shows that in groups of more than eight people, participants become withdrawn and are less likely to say what they really think. So keep the teams small. Set up a relaxed environment in a pleasant meeting room. If it's around 10.30 a.m., bring some coffee for everyone. Don't sit at the head of the table, but rather, sit at the side like everyone else does. Don't force the fact that you're the leader on people. If you're worth your salt, they will be more likely to respect you for being one of them than they will for being their boss. Ask as many simple questions as you can think of. And take notes.

I recommend asking lots of dumb questions. You can only get away with asking dumb questions during your first 90 days. After that, you're expected to know the answers. And even if you think you know the answers, keep asking. Asking questions shows that you're interested in the challenges your people face. And who knows, you might learn something.

Repeat this exercise with customers if you can. Get out and talk to as many as possible. In one of my leadership roles we tried something new. I was just three or four weeks into the job when we invited a group of customers to come and meet with the new guy — me — and tell us what they thought.

Contrary to your expectations, it was extremely constructive. Sure, you are always going to get some negative people who can't let go of an old problem. But everyone else was delighted to be invited, they were respectful of the opportunity, and we generated fantastic and helpful feedback. And we created some long-term alliances. All because we asked them what they thought.

In fact, the process was so successful that we repeated it with different customers every three months.

During these first few weeks you need to be the sponge, soaking up all the information you can. You should try talking to as many people from as many different vantage points as possible while you are in information-capture mode. Look for opportunities to get the opinions of people you wouldn't normally get to. I once took the chance to talk to a couple of truck drivers who delivered our products. They were waiting to be unloaded, and I wandered over to chat. They didn't even work for us, in fact they were contractors and I soon found out that they delivered some of our competitor's product as well. I learned a few valuable things about what was happening in the market that we weren't even aware of.

You can only get away with asking **dumb questions** for the **first 90 days.** **After that**, you're expected to **know the answers.**

As you go through these various discussions with your team members, their teams, your customers and your suppliers, you learn a lot about the business you've just become responsible for. You'll learn more in four weeks of 'management by wandering around' than any other way I know. You will, most likely, have discarded almost everything you were told in the interview. As a result, you have now built your own knowledge base.

Make sure you take good notes as you go through the process and refer to them over and over again in the coming months. First impressions are invariably accurate and you shouldn't forget them.

Your dumb questions will help you to build up your own early SWOT (strengths, weaknesses, opportunities, and threats) analysis. What are we good at? Where are we weak? Where are the opportunities? What are the threats? Who are our good people? Who's struggling? You will quickly develop a well thought out list of what your priorities will be during the rest of your first 90 days.

Make sure you communicate your findings to your key people and, in doing so, give them the opportunity to challenge you. It's important for them to understand what you are trying to achieve, so they can support your aspirations and actions.

You might get some criticism for not making enough visible progress in the first 30 days. There are always those looking for the immediate magic — the instant action that is going to change the world. In my experience, those who see action as an end in itself, rather than simply a means by which to accomplish things, are usually ill informed and have their own agenda. Irrespective of where those people sit in the organisation, ignore them and get on with your own focused process.

Incidentally, you don't have to wait to develop your master plan before starting to do things. Use the project planning forms (see Chapter 5, 'The power of planning') to get some activities going where importance and urgency converge. The cool thing about these planning templates is that they give you a means by which to demonstrate an action-oriented approach, and you are sharing the accountability from the start.

Get the first 30 days right and the next 60 days will fly by. You will, if you spend your first 90 days wisely, achieve more, do so faster and be more accurate. Take your time, ask dumb questions and listen to the people who can help you to be successful.

* * *

You have to be
20% better
every year,
just to **stay the same**.

Change — the leader's constant companion

'We always seem to be in change mode. Why can't we just settle down for a while, for a year or so, and stop trying to change things all the time?'

Team member
Telstra Media
Australia

The quote above comes from a member of one of the teams in Telstra Australia during a consultancy project that I was involved with a couple of years back. To be fair to the person concerned, it's not the first time I have heard such a comment. In fact, it's something that many of us hear regularly. A lot of our people, particularly those who have been around for a while, are sick of change. Over it. However, unfortunately for them, we can't do much about it. As leaders, we don't have much choice.

I have developed a saying that I use a lot. It goes like this:

'You have to be 20% better every year, just to stay the same.'

In other words, we need to be constantly improving, just to meet the expectations of our people and our customers; 20% better, just to maintain your position in the marketplace or to retain your relationships with your most important clients, or satisfy your shareholders. In the words of the slogan adopted by the 2012 British Olympic team, 'Better never stops'.

I'm referring to the need to constantly enhance your offer, improve your own personal performance, develop your people, and upgrade your relationship with your clients as well as the many other things that we all have to do in our daily lives.

You see, every time you or your team interact with your customers, suppliers, bank manager, debtors and others, you are setting or resetting their expectations of you. If you continually do a great job, their expectations of you will gradually continue to increase. As soon as you fail to meet those expectations, they will be disappointed. When that happens they start looking for alternatives.

Change puts pressure on everyone. Leaders, managers and the people in the

... if we don't **keep changing**,
if we don't **keep improving**,
if we don't **keep innovating**,
then we'll **go out of business**.

Bill Gates

team. Nothing puts a leadership team under as much pressure as the need to drive major change or rapid transformation within the business. The constant questioning around what you are doing, why you are doing it and why the old ways were better, mean that as the leader, you need to be very clear about the programme ahead of you, reasons for it, and the benefit of the ultimate outcomes.

Change is about getting the people within the organisation to change their habits. That can be tough to do. In fact, if you accept my view that the majority of businesses should be in change mode most, if not all, of the time, then you are constantly asking your people to change the way they go about their role. So you'd better have a good reason to do so.

Change is now a leader's only strategic certainty. Adapting to, understanding the implications of, and maximising the opportunity offered by change are all important if we want to continue to improve the performance of our team, our product or the company as a whole. But to capitalise on change you will, more often than not, need to get your people to change their habits.

The need for change comes to us for a variety of reasons and in a wide range of guises. Sometimes you will have identified a need of the business as part of your plan. Other times it is forced on you. Think about some of the things that will bring forward the need to change.

1. The most common initiator of the need for change will be a weakening **financial performance**. Irrespective of whether the issues are of your making, shareholders and superiors will want you to cut costs, find cheaper ways of doing things or grow margins and revenues, and if you are in a corporate environment they will demand that you do so quickly.

2. The other obvious source of the need for change is the introduction of **new technologies**. Whether it's the small business implementation of MYOB or Xero accounting systems, the introduction of the Salesforce CRM, or in a bigger business an SAP integration, we all have to keep up with today's new technology. While we all understand the reasons for introducing such upgrades, given the disruption in doing so it is often difficult to keep the team convinced of the benefits as you go through the process.

3. For many businesses, the **changing landscape** means simply that our businesses have to do different stuff a different way. Think about the media, telecoms, household appliances, or photographic industries and what they have been through over the last few years. None of us want to have 'a Kodak moment', where we wake up and find that we are no longer relevant.

Driving change is about getting the **people** within the organisation to **change their habits.** Think about what is required to change any habit. People first need to **understand why.** It then takes **time, motivation** and **constant reminders.**

4. The introduction of **legislation** can sometimes force change upon us. Consider the recent growing emphasis on health and safety, or employment law, or the pressure to develop and live up to diversity policies and equality of remuneration. I have no doubt that we will continue to see increased pressure on business at every level in regard to all of these issues.

5. In recent years we have seen the need to dramatically alter our approach to marketing as **new 'enablers'** have forced business to change the way it goes about things. The first of these enablers was the internet, but Google, Facebook, Twitter and others are constantly shifting the landscape and a business has to change its behaviour if it wants to be noticed. Today, between 40 and 50% of small businesses in the USA, UK, Australia and New Zealand don't have a website. And for mid-sized businesses, between 15 and 30% still fail to have a web presence.

6. **Competitor performance** remains a common reason for a business to have to lift its game and change the way it does things. Unfortunately, almost every case I see involved the business 'reacting' in a manner that is too little and too late. If your competitors are regularly beating you, or you have lost your competitive advantage for whatever reason — it may be a product change, a pricing change or the loss of key personnel — you need to get on to it quickly and make changes that will feel massive (but in reality aren't) and make them quickly.

7. Sometimes, our **customers** will demand that we change the way we do things. This can even extend to major customers requiring us to adapt to their systems, or suggesting that we buy out another business that would complement our current offering. It's not unusual today for customer demands to push the boundaries of our existing capabilities.

8. Occasionaly, we will have to deal with the one change that can cause the most angst among our people. The outcome of either **acquiring or being acquired** will inevitably mean that things will need to be done differently. In addition to aligning the operating approaches of the newly merged entities will also, in many cases, be the need to cope with increased debt levels as a result of the acquisition, and the desire to quickly get costs down and the predicted economies of scale up.

9. Last but not least, there are what I call the various **'incident'-based initiators** of change. Some result from a missed opportunity or target and the need for urgent action as a result. Some arrive simply through product changes or the arrival of new personnel. At the extreme, organisations have change programmes forced upon them as a result of an often-invasive consulting process, which invariably means your people are offside even before you start trying to adapt.

A **change leader** needs to create an **environment** in which people **understand the goals** and the **reasons for the change**. **Nobody** ever **supports** something they **don't understand**.

Whichever way the change process arises, it's important to think about the impact it will have on your people and how to enhance your chances of successfully bringing people along with you. Change programmes are about asking people to change the way they do things, or at least how to do different things. Remember, you're asking them to change their daily work habits.

Accordingly, communicating the changes or the plan or the process once and then expecting your people to follow every prescription is, I'm afraid, a recipe for failure.

Just think for a moment about the steps you must take to change any other habit. Changing your diet, quitting smoking or getting off the couch to embark on an exercise programme all require significant personal effort and a changed mind-set. To succeed you must constantly revisit your goals or aspirations and keep asking yourself, 'Why am I doing this?' You need a clear plan of what to do each day and you must constantly monitor your performance against that plan and those goals. You will fail if you don't.

It's no different in business. Asking people to change their workplace habits is a very personal request. Fail to get the request and the process right and your people will rapidly revert to old habits, quicker than you can say 'I give up'.

A change leader therefore needs to create an environment in which people understand the goals, the reasons for them and the plan required to achieve change. Take these steps and your people might feel they can get on board with your programme.

It's most important to help your team understand the reasons for the change. Nobody ever supports something that they don't understand. In the midst of new-project frustration, we've all heard the comment, 'I don't know why we are doing this . . .'

Your people will, in my experience, be incredibly supportive if they understand what you are trying to do, your reasons for doing it, and how they can play a role in the successful transition. So you need some questions to start the conversation. If everyone in your enterprise can answer these types of questions, there's a good chance your people can play a positive and constructive part in the change process. As a starting point I suggest that you get out among your team and start answering the following for them:

1. What are we trying to do?
2. Why are we doing it?
3. What will we do differently?

Talk to **lots of people**.

Ask **good questions**.

Take **good notes**.

Keep referring back to what
you have learned.

Your views are forming.

Don't worry if those **views** are **different** to
everything else that you have been told.

No one else has done what you are doing.

4. How will this plan help us achieve our goals or overcome our problem?
5. What is my role in making the changes?
6. What will my role look like at the end of this?
7. How will we know when we've succeeded?
8. Who's in charge of the process?
9. Who do I talk to if I am having trouble?

Doing this once won't be enough. It is no different to the new diet or going to the gym. People must be continuously reminded why they are doing this stuff to prevent them from falling back on old habits. As someone once said, '**Repetition is the mother of success**'.

The lessons in the following chapters will help you to meet the needs of your people as you seek to garner their support for the smaller changes you are making or the major transformation programme. Disciplines around clarity of purpose, communication, people-management processes and personally acting in a manner that is consistent with what you are trying to achieve are all important components of a successful change programme.

It's this **simple** ...
You can't **accomplish the dream** if
everyone isn't **dreaming** the
same thing every day.
Nightmares follow.

LeBron James
NBA basketball player

CHAPTER 4

'C' Words to Keep You on Course

'Start with good people, lay out the rules, communicate with your employees, motivate them and reward them. If you do all those things effectively, you can't miss.'

Lee Iacocca
Former CEO, US auto industry

I often say that good leaders change lives for the better. Successful leaders know where and how to lead people, and will often make a substantial impact on the lives of those they lead. On the other hand, good people are invariably the making of successful leaders.

I intend to explain in some detail why people are a company's most valuable asset and how, therefore, they should be treated as such. But for the moment, I want to explain why the creation of the 7 Principles of Profit was such an important milestone on my leadership journey and how you too can turn them to your advantage.

When I came out of the Stanford University Executive Programme, there were a couple of things that surprised me.

Firstly, although my New Zealand-based business experience up until that point was relatively 'small' compared to my classmates from US industry, that experience was highly relevant. In fact, it was perhaps more relevant to the broader challenges of leadership and management than that of many executives stuck in the narrow silos of big corporates. Learning from the 'bottom up', placing the ads, making sales, paying the accounts and responding to customer queries turned out to be a whole lot more useful than spending a lifetime stuck in the Treasury team.

Leaders change **lives.**

Good leaders change lives **for the better.**

Great leaders permanently **enhance the opportunities** in life that their people can pursue.

Secondly, the Stanford programme gave me the structure and the language to understand that I knew more than I thought I did and, most importantly, how to communicate it.

Many years later, when I developed the 7 Principles, they provided that same structure.

The principles are effectively my fail-proof leadership compass. They provide the structure around which to develop my thinking and my plans. They also provide the direction and framework to help me make sense of today's increasingly complex and often seriously battered organisational landscape. As I've said, people are essential because they, more than any other component of an enterprise, are responsible for ensuring that all the stakeholders have a great experience and benefit from the performance of the organisation.

But a team, no matter how talented and dedicated, can't reach the ultimate levels of performance and profit without knowing exactly where they are going, why they are doing so and how to get there. That knowledge and understanding is what I call 'clarity of purpose'. A leader's first responsibility, therefore, is to determine, articulate, communicate and consistently ensure that everyone on board the good ship enterprise knows exactly where they are going, why they are going there, and how their own role plays a part in that. I call these my three 'C' words: Clarity, Communication and Consistency.

Just as the pointers of my 7 Principles of Profit compass have guided me, so they will also help you negotiate the leadership world's often tricky terrain. Overlay them with the three 'C' words above and you will start to change the lives of the people you work with. Let me explain.

* * *

Be **clear** about what you

are trying to **achieve**.

'C' word' #1: Clarity

'Be clear about what you are trying to achieve.'

Organisations fail for just two reasons. The first is pretty obvious. A lack of appropriate financial management and control often kills an otherwise good business, run by good people. So, you have to be on top of your financials. That won't surprise too many people. The problem is that numerous managers aren't. I recently encountered a business whose latest available financial information was two months old. But I digress . . .

The second reason for failure is less obvious. It's what I call a lack of 'clarity of purpose'. In other words, organisations fail because they are not clear about what they are trying to achieve. Clarity of purpose involves being clear about what the leaders and the business as a whole are collectively trying to achieve. It involves being able to state clearly to all stakeholders — customers, suppliers, bankers and the entire team, sometimes even your family — your 'purpose' for being.

Just how clear do you have to be? The story below is 20 years old now, but it remains one of the best examples I know.

In the late 1990s I went to a day of seminars presented by a range of leaders and commentators, most of whom hailed from the United States. The line-up included former Hewlett-Packard boss and future US presidential candidate Carly Fiorina. Auckland's most commonly used large-scale conference venue was, at the time, a large cold concrete edifice out in the suburbs, into which the organisers packed about 3000 eager participants. I think we listened to six speakers that day. The highlight was undoubtedly an hour-long presentation on leadership by the late General 'Stormin'' Norman Schwarzkopf, leader of the Allied effort in what is now referred to as 'Gulf War I'. Schwarzkopf, the star of the day, was a big, imposing man — and I imagine even more so when in uniform — who spoke about the leadership and management of troops in the first war to enter our living rooms daily, courtesy of Cable News Network, or CNN.

I remember much of what he said, including some of his quotes. He was animated as he explained his three simple rules for leading teams, which were:

1. ***When placed in command, take charge!***
2. ***Do what's right!***
3. ***When in doubt, refer to rules 1 and 2!***

'OUR MISSION:

TO KICK IRAQ

OUT OF KUWAIT!'

US General
Norman Schwarzkopf

However, the highlight was yet to come. Unlike most celebrity-style speakers, Schwarzkopf ended his presentation by offering to take questions from the floor. A few of the guys in the audience asked the obvious 'blokey' questions:

'How many aircraft did you have?'

'How many troops were there?'

'What did the war cost?'

'How many casualties were there?'

'How many troops did you lose?'

'Why didn't you go all the way into Baghdad and kill Saddam Hussein?'

. . . plus a few more. I'm sure you get the idea.

Then a woman in the middle of the hall stood up and, in front of those 3000 people, asked her own absolutely brilliant question:

'General,' she said, 'how do you manage a team of 800,000 people?'

The crowd went totally silent. I sat there thinking, 'I wish I had asked that.'

The General's answer was no less brilliant!

*'Oh,' he said. 'Managing 800,000 people was easy. You see, we only had one goal — **to kick Iraq out of Kuwait**.' His statement was made with a confidence and certainty that indicated he'd used the same phrase many times before.*

He continued: 'So if we had transport problems, logistics problems, dietary problems, accommodation problems, religious problems — and we had all of those — we knew that those problems were not going to be an issue unless they affected our ability to kick Iraq out of Kuwait!'

*The General became even more animated and added: 'And every member of that 800,000-person team knew what we were there to do. They all carried a card in their backpack which stated: '**Our mission: to kick Iraq out of Kuwait**.' He repeated the phrase six or seven times during his answer. He was clearly still passionate about the goal, even though a few years had passed since the war was over.*

Here's my point. The General had provided clarity of purpose to every one of those 800,000 people that were part of his team. That was his key to managing 800,000 people. It was absolutely clear. There was no room for question or doubt. It was easy to communicate and easily understood. He had clearly made the statement over and over again, probably hundreds of times in all. And most of all, it was not easy to back away from.

More recent examples include Facebook's stated purpose: 'To give people the power to share and make the world more open and connected.'

Most people go to **work** every day and do what they

THINK

they are **meant to do.**

Google seeks to 'organise the world's information'. Amazon's stated aim is 'to be Earth's most customer-centric company, where customers can find and discover anything at Amazon.com'.

I'm not suggesting that it's always straightforward or simple to identify your purpose and come up with a concise phrase that captures it. But you need to try to get this kind of clarity if you want your customers to understand what you're all about, and get your people to deliver it.

* * *

Are you making noise or music?

*Imagine a group of 20 people singing whatever they want to sing. Each individual is singing his or her favourite song, in their own time and their own key. Imagine the cacophony: **noise**.*

*Now imagine the same group singing one song, together! They start together, know the words, sing in the same key and harmonise. Singing 'from the same hymn sheet' makes **music**.*

* * *

Around 85% of businesses don't have a plan, according to Harvard Business Review (HBR) research findings. Given my experiences, I believe them. As a result, most organisations are busy making noise rather than music, and their people aren't sure what song they should be singing.

Most people in most businesses have little or no idea what the organisation they work for is trying to achieve. Even the few businesses that have a plan don't think to tell their people what it is. The majority of businesses comprise groups of well-intentioned people doing their thing, reacting to what occurs, to their own personal standard and timeframe, and hoping that the results will be good enough to keep them employed. As logic would dictate, the businesses and their people both underachieve.

For some reason, managers and business owners are often reluctant to share information with their people. Your people must be given the benefit of the doubt. Tell them what's going on. Very few people go to work to do a bad job. Most go to work every day and do what they THINK is required of them.

Our goal is to have our people come to work every day and do what they

KNOW

they are **meant to do.**

Let's go back to the music analogy. Leaders like you must, I believe, write the music, modify the score, arrange the players and conduct the orchestra. You also need to guide the band as they seek to get better. I've seen countless examples of small, medium and large businesses, and even voluntary organisations, crammed with people doing what they genuinely believe is the right thing to do. But the actions and outcomes bear no resemblance to the organisation's objectives.

When your people KNOW what they're meant to do, the impact is dramatic. This clarity plays out as increased productivity, happier customers, better financial performance and, in my experience, a happier, more innovative and higher-energy workplace. And something else happens. Management starts getting useful feedback from the front line about what's working and what's not. Why? Because people know what's important.

Recently, I led a consulting project within a large public organisation that was failing in a high-profile manner. On my first day, I joined the 12-person management team for their weekly meeting. As my project was introduced to them, I asked my standard opening question.
'Tell me what we are trying to achieve,' I asked.
I received 12 different answers.

As in the example above, when I get involved in a new business for the first time, I often ask people in the team, including the leaders, what they are trying to achieve.

You'd be surprised how often business owners, managers, leaders and even CEOs and directors of major companies can't answer that question. Many big businesses get dumb and lazy, and so this probably doesn't come as any great surprise. But the reality does present a great improvement opportunity.

But it's the plight of the small to medium-sized businesses that really staggers me. Here, owners go through all the pain of running a business, paying the bills, borrowing money, dealing with banks, employing people and, in many cases, they're working 60, 70 or even 80 hours a week. And yet, they still can't explain in a simple straightforward way what they are doing it for. So much for the frankly illusionary freedom of self-employment.

No enterprise leader can afford to start a day, month or year without a clear plan of what he or she is trying to accomplish. Many people stumble into businesses or, in some cases, inherit them. Either way, if you find yourself in this predicament, it's best to get on and make the most of it.

So,
what are you
trying to achieve?

In search of 'clarity of purpose'

So, where do you start seeking clarity? How do you go about it? The later chapter on business planning will help you. But in the meantime, here are some thoughts to get you started.

We now know that an effective leader must be absolutely clear about what he or she is trying to achieve. I warn you, however, that seeking clarity is a multi-dimensional question that must be answered over time. It's not simply about the products being sold or the profits the enterprise is trying to generate.

Examples of the questions that need to be answered in pursuit of clarity include:

1. What is your ultimate long-term goal? (Some examples that I have seen include: make a lot of money, have a lifestyle, have fun, have 1000 customers, make a difference, sell the business, change the employment prospects of 100 people, have the highest- performing team in the company, create opportunities for future generations of the family, meet long-term growth targets, etc.)
2. Can you break the goal down into one-month, three-month and 12-month objectives?
3. What key business components (product mix, pricing, talent, customer mix, etc.) are required to enable us to reach the goal?
4. What type of organisation or team do you want to develop?
5. In an ideal world, how will your people behave?
6. Do you want to employ people or work alone?
7. How will you treat customers? (Are you 'high value-add' or 'pile it high and sell it cheap'?)
8. How will you treat your people? (What sort of working environment do you wish to create?)

You will, from time to time, need to ask hundreds of questions like this. To get started you only need a few. You'll be surprised what clarity this process brings.

I'm now, as you may be able to see, heading towards business plans, mission and values statements and the like. You will read all about the importance of how to tackle business planning later. In the meantime, I simply want to point out that these questions and others like them will play an important part in the clarity of purpose process and the communication that follows. And this stuff applies whether you're running a major corporation or a one-person business, a little league sports team or, dare I say it, a family!

Try some blue sky thinking . . . assuming that you don't own the company . . .

What would you do differently if you owned the business?

CLARITY IS A PLAN'S CORNERSTONE

Once you establish a clear purpose, it should become the cornerstone upon which your entire business plan, and often your business philosophy, is built. Seeking that clarity should be the very first step in your business planning process. And the many steps that follow should all relate in some way to that core purpose.

Listed below are some actions and questions you should consider as you go through a typical business planning session.

- Describe your company values.
- How would you describe your company culture?
- Do you have a clear mission statement that is understood by your people?
- Describe your strengths, weaknesses, opportunities, and threats.
- What are the major issues affecting your success?
- What are your top five business priorities today?
- Do you have the right people on board to help reach your goals?
- What do your customers think of you?
- What do you want your customers to think of you?

These are all pretty standard business planning questions and suggestions. But I hope you can see that unless you are really clear about what you are trying to achieve, the answers to many of these questions become irrelevant. They simply won't relate to anything.

*For example, let's say you're running a discount jewellery business and you sell high-turnover, low-quality, low-price, low-margin products. As the saying goes you, 'pile it high and sell it cheap'. Privately, your main purpose is to sell as much product and make as much money as possible. Publicly, you might put a marketing spin on it and state your purpose as being **'for every person to be able to own inexpensive jewellery'**. The decisions that flow from this purpose and positioning might include: You'll probably operate a basic store in a secondary location. You won't, in all likelihood, pay your people a lot, put too much effort into their product training or employment conditions, and you won't worry too much about loyalty, happily letting people stay or go.*

*Alternatively, let's now imagine that you are managing a more up-market jewellery store. You sell a small quantity of high-value, high-quality items at a high margin. Your core purpose might be **'to help people celebrate special occasions in a memorable way'**. In this case, delivering outstanding customer service, harbouring values such as integrity and trust and maintaining absolute*

Have you ever played tennis?

In the game of tennis, one of the basic skills is knowing where to stand on the court. Ideally, you should always be in one of two places. Option one is to be on the baseline, from where you have time to see the ball and get into position to make your shot. Alternatively, you should be up close to the net where you can quickly volley your return of the ball, giving your opponent less time to react. If you are standing anywhere in between, it becomes difficult because you are likely to be positioned close to where the ball is landing — so it bounces at your feet and is difficult to hit. This area is called '**no-man's-land**'.

Business is similar. You need to be clear about your position in the market. Are you selling high volumes of low-price product, with low margins and low value add? Or, alternatively, are you selling select items, in small quantities, of high-quality, high-priced product, with high levels of customer service and value add?

Anywhere in between will be difficult to execute and even more difficult for your customer to understand. In other words, '**no-man's-land**'.

confidentiality will be critical to your success. Your approach to recruiting, training, remunerating and retaining your key personnel will be totally different.

Each of the two approaches to business is okay. There is no indication that one is right and one is wrong. There is room in the market for both offerings. However, the answers to the list of questions above will be different in each of the two scenarios. Your ability to be clear about your purpose, or what you are trying to achieve, means that you will respond differently to the various management challenges and, therefore, make decisions that are absolutely consistent with those objectives.

∗ ∗ ∗

REAL CLARITY MEANS EASIER DECISION-MAKING

Now consider this. Time after time, I see organisations get distracted from the key opportunities in their business. Today, emails, phone messages, social media, online sales offers, increasing competition, cheap imports, and dodgy characters turning up in person or online, all compete for our attention. My solution to this clutter is simple: 'clarity of purpose'. The clearer you are about where you are going and what you want to achieve, the less distracted you will be by activities of the crazy, attention-seeking world that surrounds you.

Most business people spend too much time being distracted from their core activities. A clear purpose, well communicated, highlights what's important and where you and your team need to be spending your time. In other words, as you become more clear about your purpose, your goals and key objectives, then decision-making becomes more straightforward. The reason is that the right decisions become more obvious once you shut out the various distractions that are brought about by a confused direction or a lack of focus.

So, if you are making decisions about the type of people you need to employ, or the location of your office or warehouse, or key customers to target, the greater the clarity overall, the easier those decisions become.

Let's return for a moment to the jewellery business.

Imagine being offered the purchase of a high-quality $30,000 gem at a wholesale price. Now let's say you're running the first 'pile them high and sell them cheap' store. The decision is easy. You won't be interested in buying this precious rock.

If, on the other hand, you're running the second store, the high-quality

If you are **really clear** about what you are **trying to achieve, decision-making** becomes much **easier**.

retailer in the High Street showroom, you're almost certainly going to buy that beautiful bauble. You're crystal clear on what your business is about and you understand what's important to your business and your clients. Clarity of purpose makes your decision dead easy and determines your behaviour.

The value of clarity as it relates to planning is not limited to retailers.

My experience in publishing reminds me that the best media brands are very clear on their offer and focus on a distinctly defined audience of both readers and advertisers. As a result, good programming or editorial decisions are easier to make. In this part of the world, Cosmopolitan magazine has a very different positioning and target audience to that of the Australian Women's Weekly. The differences are obvious to the reader in everything from the cover image to the fashion and beauty pages. While there will be some overlap, magazine buyers will purchase one or the other, reflecting their stage of life and their interests. Similarly, different advertisers will use these publications to position their products as being suitable for the target audience of the chosen media, in this case the younger woman versus the more mature woman. Media brands that try to be all things to all people struggle because their target market is not able to clearly recognise the connection.

Similarly, the best real estate agents focus on a defined geographical territory, type of property or specific price range. The best swimming teachers are unlikely to coach Olympic swimmers, while Olympic coaches don't teach beginners to swim. Clarity delivers specialisation and focus, and that's what delivers success.

So don't just start those planning days with a SWOT analysis and questions about values and mission statements. Think instead about why you're even in business. This key question, by the way, applies equally to the business you're running as it does to the career you're trying to manage. And, when you stop to think about it, it applies just as well to the management and leadership of your family, your daily health and fitness routine, and even your relationships with your kids.

So, at the risk of repeating myself again, before you start to plan anything, answer the question: 'What are we trying to achieve?'

SUMMARY: JUST ONE MORE THING

What's a desirable side effect? In my experience, such clarity helps you to engage your people, sell more products and generate happier customers. And don't worry too much if you can't package your purpose into a slick phrase like those global corporate examples mentioned earlier. A few descriptive bullet points are just as effective.

We all have less than ideal experiences with the businesses we deal with. Poor

The following is from the text of the children's classic Alice in Wonderland. *The exchange occurs as Alice comes to a fork in the road, and is between Alice and the Cheshire Cat.*

Alice: Would you please tell me which way I ought to go from here?

Cat: That depends a good deal on where you want to get to.

Alice: I don't much care where.

Cat: Then it doesn't matter which way you go.

Lewis Carroll
Alice in Wonderland

service, inadequate follow-up, time delays, and so on. I'm a customer, trying to give money to at least one business or group of people every day. Yet they frequently do a lousy job of taking my money in return for the provision of good service.

Every day I encounter someone answering a phone who doesn't have a pen or paper with which to take a message. Every day I encounter a service provider who could have done a better job dealing with my needs. How often do you leave a restaurant and say: 'WOW, that was the best experience it could have been'? Rarely, right? Something can always be done better, usually much better. There's always plenty of room for improvement.

Being absolutely clear about what you are trying to achieve, and communicating it effectively, is the first step on the journey to giving customers that 'wow' experience and, as a result, running a successful operation. If, as General Schwarzkopf said, it works for the military, chances are it will work for you and your team.

In my experience, clarity permeates through an organisation. It affects the way you talk about the business and it positively impacts the actions of the people you interact with on a daily basis — most notably your team, suppliers and customers.

* * *

Postscript: 10 reasons why organisations fail

1. The leadership is not clear about what they are trying to achieve.
2. Values ascribed to the organisation are not reflected by the behaviour of the managers and leaders.
3. A lack of teamwork means that everyone is working on their own thing without understanding how that thing aligns to the objectives of the organisation.
4. Senior managers fail to identify and accept problems early enough and as a result fail to respond in a timely manner.
5. The people within the business are not fully informed, and as a result they react, doing what they think they are meant to do, rather than being in a position to know what they are meant to do.
6. A failure to express the roles of the people in a way that helps those people understand why their role is important and how it contributes to the overall objectives of the company.
7. Remuneration structures do not align with business objectives. (It sounds obvious, doesn't it?)
8. Having set the expectations regarding standards of performance among their colleagues and their customers, the leaders themselves fail to meet those expectations.
9. There is an unrealistic expectation that the customer will understand what you are talking about.
10. A lack of appropriate financial management and control.

With the exception of item 10, all of these issues are a function of the failure of item 1.

The single biggest problem in **communication** is the **illusion** that it has **taken place**.

George Bernard Shaw
Playwright
Nobel Prize winner

'C' word' #2: Communication

'Communicate, communicate, communicate.'

Whatever your leadership style, good leaders must be good communicators. Clear, consistent and compelling communication is to successful leadership what location, location, location is to real estate riches. Communication is, from my experience, one of the golden rules of effective leadership. And it's critically important whenever times are tough or, alternatively, if you are in the midst of transformational change, as every organisation is these days.

Once you are clear about what you're trying to achieve, you need to start communicating the key messages to your people. In particular, you need to share information with those people who are critical to helping you achieve your objectives.

As a leader you'll be aware of the various everyday pressures that confront your company, your division or your team. The sources of these pressures vary depending on whether you are responsible for a corporation, a department or a small privately owned or family-based enterprise.

The global economy has suffered over the past few years and since the global financial crisis and its ensuing financial market meltdown. In the post-GFC world, increased uncertainty has placed added pressure on business to an extent greater than most of us has witnessed for some time.

In such circumstances, the need for improved communication within the business is at its most obvious. As leaders, we usually know the facts about the state of our businesses and the inherent risks or difficulties that the market climate might be generating. I've always believed that it's easier to cope with the heat of the moment when you know the details around the extent of the damage or difficulty.

Spare a thought, then, for those in your team who aren't in leadership roles and don't, therefore, have access to your greater level of information. These people go to work each day and perform their roles, usually to the best of their ability, but unaware of the full details about what's going on in the business. This lack of knowledge can, understandably, result in a high degree of uncertainty on the part of your people, particularly during times of economic upheaval, which, coincidentally, is when people feel most concerned about job security. So while it's always important to communicate with your people, it's an even more critical challenge for management to deal with when uncertainty exists.

In the period from 2008 to 2011 when I worked with the Yellow Pages company, it was one of many companies really feeling the combined heat of rapid technological

In a world infused with **social media**,
your people will **find out what's going on**
whether you like it or not.
It's always **better** if they
hear it from you.

change and global economic uncertainty. The company's core business, revenue generated by printed classified advertising, was deteriorating rapidly. The global financial crisis accelerated an already challenging trading environment for many of Yellow's clients.

To make matters even more difficult, the company was saddled with an unsustainable level of debt, created when it was subjected to a private equity funded acquisition at the peak of the market in 2007.

Borrowing the terminology from the well-documented hurricane that hit the North Atlantic coast in the early 1990s, we called this situation 'The Perfect Storm'. We had a combination of:

- A declining business due to structural issues created by the advance of the internet and the dominance of Google;
- The Global Financial Crisis, resulting in company failures and a mammoth (25% worldwide in the first 12 months) decline in advertising spend;
- A debt burden equal to six times revenue and 11 times EBITDA (earnings before interest, tax, depreciation, and amortization).

This 'perfect storm' worsened when the media became deeply interested in Yellow's predicament and began telling the story, often quite inaccurately. Consequently, our people were bombarded with newspaper, radio, television and online articles, which, among other things, stated that our business was in severe difficulty, was likely to be wound up, and that many people would lose their jobs.

> *'I remember that many of our people had set up "Google alerts" for news and information about our company. As I wandered around the business they would regularly approach me, concerned about the content of yet another press story and seeking my assurance that everything would be okay. In many cases, people in our sales teams were being questioned daily as to our financial viability by customers worried about advance payments for advertising.'*

It was a classic example of an act or event which puts pressure on your people, the troops, who front up every day and do a good job despite what is going on in the world around them. The risk is that without good internal communication, your people will see and read the media's coverage and assume it to be true.

Obviously, we don't all get into similarly difficult situations, but the Yellow Pages experience does highlight the need to constantly communicate with your people during difficult times. When people don't have access to information that keeps

There is only **one rule** in **communication** that **works**: 'Always assume the message **doesn't get through!**'

In other words …

Communicate

Communicate

Communicate

them accurately informed, they have no option but to rely on others, in this case the media, for information which in turn shapes their view of things.

Constantly communicating with our people in Yellow's very difficult situation was critical. We gave our people accurate details of what was actually happening to both satisfy their own curiosity and, just as importantly, that of the customers and clients whom our people were dealing with every day.

Whether you're circulating a new business plan or dealing with a public relations disaster, you must be able to deliver clear communication to your people and your other key stakeholders. For me there is just one golden rule that works when it comes to communicating with your people:

'Always assume that the message doesn't get through.'

I'll repeat my mantra: 'Communicate, communicate, communicate'. In other words, whatever your key messages are, repeat them over and over again.

The reason is simple. Unfortunately, with all the noise within most organisations, very few people get the message the first, or for that matter even the second, time.

And when there's a lot of competing information out there, you will have to repeat a message or a theme over and over again in order to drive clarity into your target audience's mind-set. The best politicians are, of course, brilliant at this. They pick up one or two key themes and repeat them ad nauseam until they think the voting public has taken their message on board. It's a lesson that those of us in business would do well to follow.

* * *

I've made this comment many times in my life. The great majority of people go to work with the intention of doing a good job. Very few intend doing a bad job. A good many are, whether they know it or not, doing a poor job. And it's not always their fault.

I have often found myself involved in a conversation about a person or group of people who are thought to be underperforming in some way. As the manager concerned outlines what is not happening, or not being done well enough, I always start by giving the person in the firing line the benefit of the doubt. So I ask the following question:

'Do they know that they are meant to be doing that?'

Most people go to work with the **intention** of doing **a good job**.

But it's **up to you** to **enable them** to do that.

For example, the universal issue that applies to most businesses — and thus most of us can identify with it — is the need to keep the office kitchen clean. I've lost count of the number of times I've seen someone scalded for the state of the company kitchen, only to ask the question above and receive a blank stare.

You can't make your people accountable unless they know what they are meant to be doing. And guess what? Most people don't, because managers don't tell them. At the risk of repeating myself, most businesses don't have a plan. Most businesses don't induct their new people. Here's how it plays out.

Recently, I called a large publicly owned utility company and asked for the CEO, whom I know, by name. The receptionist asked me what department he worked in! Our conversation went on to highlight that she was relatively new to the business and had had no induction or initial training at all. And she was answering the phones!

I believe, again through experience, in the power and capability of a team of good people. But to be effective, people need clear, unambiguous leadership. Sadly, as noted earlier, the majority of people go to work every day and do what they think they're meant to do. Imagine the impact if they went to work every day knowing exactly what they were meant to do!

Here are a couple of statistics that may, or may not, surprise you. Either way, they illustrate my point perfectly.

- On average, 95% of a company's employees are unaware of, or do not understand, their company's strategy. (HBR, October 2005)
- 90% of business strategies fail due to poor execution. (University of Adelaide Business 2 Community, 30 October 2012)

Coupled with numerous statistics like these, my views regarding internal communication are the result of my observation of hundreds of people in small, medium and large businesses. These people worked in all sorts of roles from the very junior to the most senior. I've watched them over the last 30 years doing what they guessed they needed to do, and doing it to the best of their ability. The majority of those people were, as a consequence, making a minor contribution compared to what they could potentially achieve. In some cases, and despite their best intentions, their actions had the opposite effect to what the organisation needed.

Harvard Business Review
The Office of Strategy Management

■ Study of 1854 large corporations globally.

■ Seven out of eight companies failed to achieve profitable growth.

■ 90% of the companies in the study had developed detailed strategic plans with much higher targets than they achieved.

■ 95% of a company's employees were unaware of, or did not understand, its strategy.

■ HR managers revealed that the HR strategies and remuneration (incentives) of 67% of those organisations were not aligned with business unit and corporate strategies.

■ HR and IT departmental plans do not support corporate or business-unit strategic initiatives. Budgeting is similarly disconnected.

■ Some 60% of organisations do not link their financial budgets to strategic priorities.

■ The compensation packages of 70% of middle managers and more than 90% of frontline employees have no link to the success or failure of strategy implementation.

By Robert S. Kaplan and David P. Norton

These well-intentioned endeavours do not automatically convert into success because:

i. Management is unclear about what the business is trying to achieve; or
ii. The organisation's leaders have not communicated what they're trying to achieve to their people.

There's no excuse for not being clear about an organisation's objectives. And yet, in the majority of cases that's the biggest problem. With respect to the second point, however, some managers choose to keep their people in the dark. Even in the most trying of times, leaders must trust their people with the information that allows them to understand the effectiveness of their actions. The mushroom principle of keeping people in the dark, hoping they will grow, has long since been discredited.

∗ ∗ ∗

THE DAY THAT CHANGED MY VIEW OF MANAGEMENT

While living and working in the United Kingdom, I worked for one of the large, privately held management consulting firms. The job provided a range of fantastic experiences, working to help improve corporate performance across several global businesses. One of my most memorable experiences occurred during a project I was leading at a huge financial services company.

The company was one of the major players in the finance and insurance sector in the United Kingdom and had been operating for more than 160 years. After that much time they should, I thought, know what they were doing!

Our consultancy assignment contained a number of components. The company had made several changes to their senior management ranks and we were invited to help them drive the change process. The focus was on systems, process streamlining, management structures, cost reduction and, in some cases, people rationalisation.

It's worth noting that, at the time, our client was the most hierarchical and bureaucratic organisation I'd ever laid eyes on, and it remains so to this day.

At the time of our arrival, the company had multiple backlogs and blockages, including a multi-year processing backlog for new pension applications. In other words, if you applied for a new pension three or four years previously, and despite the fact that you had been paying your automatic payments ever since, your application had not yet been processed, and thus you didn't exist in the system. Here was a large bureaucratic financial services organisation in desperate need of

Your people cannot **help you** to reach **your goals** if they **don't know** what **you are trying to achieve**.

an overhaul, and, to their credit, the new bosses were up for it.

We had a team of about 36 people working on the various projects within the company at any one time. As one of the project leaders, I spent two to three days a week in their offices. The rest of my time was spent running another project for a computer industry client. The city of Reading, in which our client's large administration centre was located, is situated 40 miles west of central London and is a mid-sized city by UK standards with a population of about 200,000 people. The city is host to a number of big-name companies across the financial services and technology sectors in particular.

The story I'm about to recount illustrates the importance of the points I've made about leadership clarity and communication. It really was the day that changed my attitude to leadership and management.

We were into week five of our assignment, which eventually ran for 18 months. It was then that I had one of those career moments you never forget. I remember the day and the incident very clearly; right down to the colour of the suit, shirt and tie I was wearing. And I will never forget the face of the young man I encountered, and around whom this story is based.

I was approached, out of the blue, by a very nervous and seemingly very young employee. Pale-skinned and spotty-faced, he appeared at first to be 18 or 19 years old. The conversation we had went something like this:

HIM: *Excuse me. Are you that Australian consultant joker?*
ME: Yes. [While I'm actually a New Zealander, I could tell from his extremely nervous demeanour that the last thing he needed right then was an antipodean geography lesson.]
HIM: *Can I talk to you for a moment?*
ME: Sure.

He froze with nervousness. As if he had thought about how to approach me, but hadn't thought much beyond that. We needed an icebreaker to steady his nerves so I introduced myself and asked him his name.

HIM: *Charlie.*
ME: *Hi, Charlie. I'm Bruce. Do you work here?*
HIM: *Yes.*
ME: *Where do you sit?*

Whatever it is that you are
trying to achieve,
you must get that **message** to
the **people** who are **interfacing**
with your customers.

Rather embarrassed, he pointed to a small desk in the open plan area, not even a cubicle, that was equipped with an in-tray and an out-tray, but no phone.

ME: *How old are you?*
HIM: *Seventeen.*
ME: *How long have you been here?*
HIM: *Eight months.*
ME: *First job?*
HIM: *Yeah!*
ME: *What do you do here?*

He was starting to warm up, but just a bit!

HIM: *My job is to check page three and four of the pension application form.*
ME: *Really? [disbelief] How long have you been doing that?*
HIM: *Eight months.*
ME: *How are you going?*
HIM: *Really well.*
ME: *How do you know?*
HIM: *I've never had any of my forms returned.*

Think about this for a moment. What's wrong with this picture?

- He's doing a boring, repetitive task.
- He's been doing the same thing for eight months without a change.
- He has limited responsibility because he's checking just two out of eight pages. (We discovered later that two other people were checking the rest of the form.)
- His only feedback mechanism was that none of his forms had been returned.
- Little did he know, the system was so messed up, he would never have received one of his forms back, even if he had made a complete mess of it.

The conversation continued:

ME: *Are you enjoying it?*
HIM: *Yeah!*
ME: *What made you come to work here?*
HIM: *I grew up here in Reading. If you live around here, there are only really*

This question should haunt

every manager:

'Can you please tell me

what we do?'

a couple of things you can do. Play football, or work in financial services. I'm not very good at football.
ME: *So this is it?*
HIM: *Yeah. Job for life.*

The UK provided my first encounter with the term 'job for life'. At the time, it seemed to be a serious consideration for many people. I suspect it still is in many cases. At the risk of being disrespectful to those who embrace the concept, I can't personally think of anything worse than a job for life. Now on with the story . . . Having made the effort to develop a rapport with Charlie, I could see his confidence growing.

ME: *So, Charlie, how can I help you?*

I will never forget his reply:

HIM: *Can you please tell me what we do?*
'Can you please tell me what we do?'

It's a question that should haunt every manager like it's haunted me ever since that day. I was, momentarily, stunned. I ran the gamut of a range of instant emotion-based responses over the next few seconds — from disbelief, surprise, pity and annoyance, before settling on a feeling of sadness.

Here was Charlie, eight months into his first job in the real world and no one had even bothered to tell him what the company did. Further questioning revealed that he had never received any induction or training or even the most basic communication about the company and what it did. Sadder still, he didn't feel comfortable about asking one of his colleagues or his boss. He waited until a less-threatening option, an outsider from the other side of the world, came along.

It transpired that his predicament was by no means unique. He was put up to approaching me by a couple of his colleagues who were in a similar pond of undesired ignorance.

My chat with Charlie remains a deeply etched and unforgettable conversation. Those five or ten minutes serve as a powerful reminder of the obligations we leaders have to communicate with our people and provide them with clarity. Charlie effectively and permanently changed my outlook on the value of good leadership and the importance of communicating with your people. All because he plucked up the nerve to ask a question.

Because he **understood more** about what the **company was trying to achieve**, Charlie was able to add **far greater value** to the **organisation** than he was previously in a position to do.

What, then, did we do about Charlie? We made an example of him. We decided to make him part of the solution. I mentioned that our client had massive processing backlogs that were costing the company a great deal in terms of both credibility with clients and financial impact. To get on top of this problem we needed to understand the processes they were currently operating. Step up, Charlie.

We sent Charlie out into the field with one of the sales reps. Once the rep sold a new pension, Charlie was instructed to take the newly signed pension application form to the first place it went for processing. He was then to tell that person that his was the highest priority pension application in the company and that it had to be processed immediately. He would then go to the next step in the process with the same instructions in terms of priority and keep doing so until he finished. He was then to return to me. We showed him how to map the process, very simply, as he went.

It took him three and a half days. This process was, at its worst, taking almost nine years! As a result of this exercise we could visualise the entire process, complete with all the bottlenecks that caused the backlogs. Charlie very quickly understood more about the business that he was part of. We drafted Charlie into our project team to help streamline the way applications were dealt with. After all, he was now the only person in the business who understood the entire process!

Charlie was soon approached by others in the company keen to have him answer their own questions about the business. As an eight-month veteran, he became part of the communication solution. And armed with his new knowledge about what his employer was trying to achieve, Charlie identified ways to improve the process and reduce the processing timeline.

Because he understood more about what the company was trying to do, Charlie could add far greater value to the business than he was ever going to accomplish checking pages three and four of the pension application form.

I often wonder what happened to Charlie. He was a good kid and I would have liked to stay in contact with him. This experience occurred before Facebook or LinkedIn enabled us to keep in touch with people. But I genuinely hope that his question, and our response, played a small part in him having a better career than he otherwise might have. I know that his question — 'Can you please tell me what we do?' — certainly changed my outlook and my career.

✳ ✳ ✳

You have to **get in front** of your **people** and tell them **what is going on**. **Speak to them** in **their language**, not yours. **Talk about the stuff that they care about**.

One of the highest priorities for any leader is to be constantly communicating with his or her people. Again it's one of those things that sounds so obvious. There's just one problem: most people in management or leadership roles don't do it.

And before you jump to your own defence and start talking about your weekly or monthly newsletter, I have some bad news for you. Your people don't read newsletters any more. They live in the Facebook era. The Google generation. The Instagram environment. The Snapchat society. Now think about this while you read the next instalment of the company newsletter. Have I convinced you yet?

* * *

So how do you get the message out? We leaders have several options, many of them provided by new technologies developed over the last few years. These include messages on the company website, intranet message boards or even using social media such as Facebook or Twitter. You can set up a programme of regular emails or newsletters. Each option has its place and should be utilised regularly, particularly when it's a frequent 'business as usual' communication.

But nothing really beats the **big room meeting**. If you can regularly get all your people together in one room and speak with them, you should. In my opinion, face-to-face communication is best. You'll still have to repeat your messages from time to time. But the big room meeting allows you to tell your story with the force of your own personality to emphasise the importance of each point. Your personality or sense of importance is often lost in the printed word or news item.

You can also see the reaction from your people when you present face to face. You can observe the body language and gauge whether they're referring your comments to their colleagues. You can, by reading the mood in the room, soften or modify your message to enhance impact or understanding. Most importantly, the big room meeting facilitates interaction. You create an environment in which people can ask questions. They won't always ask questions in front of their peers, but you can still create an environment that allows them to talk with you in small groups or even one-on-one sessions. You can also invite them to email questions to you.

Some of you might recall or have read about superstar American CEO Lee Iacocca when he was attempting to rescue his country's struggling car manufacturer, Chrysler Corporation, back in the 1980s. Iacocca used what he called 'town hall meetings'. He travelled to cities throughout the United States, where Chrysler employed thousands of people, to talk to them openly about

Big room meetings with **all** of
your **people** in attendance provide
the **best opportunity** for
unfiltered communication.

the challenges facing the company. He could, in his own words, tell his people directly what was going on.

Despite the publication of pages and pages of bad press and the broadcasting of countless hours of television journalism, all of which threatened to topple the iconic company, Iacocca was able to get the message out to his people. And it worked because his people heard his version of events straight from the top and they believed him. As a result, Iacocca and his people rescued Chrysler, admittedly with the help of a $US1.5 billion loan from the US Treasury, which was subsequently fully repaid.

Faced with the same issues, a modern-day Iacocca would, I'm sure, use email, Facebook, Twitter, websites, and even YouTube videos to get his or her message across. Nevertheless, these new forms of communication should be used alongside the big room meeting, not instead of it.

$$* * *$$

While I've focused so far on communication in difficult times, the same approach is relevant to almost all of your organisational messaging. Whether you are communicating a business plan, a new product launch, a marketplace success story, celebrating a result of some sort, or celebrating one of your people, try to think of all the things you can do to constructively and positively get messages, of whatever kind, out to all your stakeholders.

Good communication is, of course, a two-way street. Good leaders want and need to hear the views of the people they send their messages to. As a leader, you need to create opportunities to hear from your various audiences. One of the most effective ways I've developed to hear from my people is to have **regular morning teas** with different teams within the organisation. I suggest meeting up with no more than eight people at a time. Any more than that and people become reluctant to speak openly.

My rule for these get-togethers is simple: I bring the muffins and the team brings the agenda. I also prefer to go to them in their space. You are immediately opening yourself up to your people and providing a comfortable setting in which they can raise issues that are important to them. Don't expect it to all go smoothly from the start. It takes time for the word to get around that you're sufficiently approachable to discuss whatever your people want to raise.

I accept, regrettably, that most managers are reluctant to risk exposing themselves

Sit down with **your people**
in **small groups** and **ask them**
what they **want to talk about**.

to these sorts of meetings. My experience suggests that managers are generally fearful of what people might ask for and, more to the point, what that request might cost. The reality is quite different. After almost 20 years running these small group sessions with my teams, the most expensive thing my people asked for came about as a result of a request by one of our magazine designers during a morning tea.

In this case our female employees, who frequently worked late on deadlines, wanted an additional night light at the entrance to the office car park. It cost $1,178.00 and instantly resolved a serious security issue. It was an issue that I would not have been aware of but for the communication opportunity created by our morning teas.

People always appreciate good open communication. Face time with the boss is valuable to both parties. As the leader, you get to put your message across in a personal and, hopefully, trustworthy manner. A lot of people will say that they don't have time for this stuff. Believe me, the added productivity for you, your team and your organisation make the time commitment more than worthwhile. More importantly, you get to hear what your people are thinking and saying.

* * *

STOPPING THE CHATTER

I used to be on a school board. Like many schools, we had our share of car park chatter. You know the sort of stuff. Parents, after dropping their kids at school in the morning, standing around the car park or meeting in the coffee shop across the road, discussing things they were dissatisfied with at the school. Things like car parking, the quality of sports grounds, a particular teacher, and so on.

Resorting to my morning tea theory I suggested to the Principal that we use the weekly school newsletter to invite parents to meet her for a chat.

'Wednesday morning teas,' we wrote. 'The Principal will be available every Wednesday morning at 9 a.m. to meet parents in the coffee shop across the road from the school. Please come along and share your thoughts and ideas and any feedback you may have.'

Guess what happened? You are probably thinking that no one turned up. But, in the first week about 19 people turned up and, predictably, talked

Create the **opportunity** for your **people** to **openly share their views** and the water cooler pity parties will go away.

about car parking, sports fields, teacher quality, and so on. The second week came and about nine people showed up. By week four, two or three people came along just for a chat. Soon the Principal was drinking coffee on her own. And the car park chatter? That died away too.

Give people the opportunity to share their views, speak their mind or simply hear your version of events, and the chances are they'll be more satisfied with things. Irrespective of the type of business you're in, creating opportunities to speak openly with small groups of people can be highly valuable.

You can now, I hope, appreciate why I believe good communication is vital to effective leadership. I'm not sure why, but many people in leadership roles have some difficulty developing and implementing an effective way of communicating that works. So I hope the experiences and approaches I've outlined above are helpful.

✳ ✳ ✳

SUMMARY: SIX SIMPLE COMMUNICATION SUGGESTIONS

Here are some simple things that you can do to improve the quality and regularity of your communication within the business. These things have all worked really well for me in the past.

1. **Move your desk to open plan**

    I've sat in open plan offices for 20 years. I can't believe that in 2017 executives are still hiding themselves away in their own inaccessible offices. Getting out of your office and sitting among the troops will, more than any other single action, have the greatest positive impact on your communication, and in the shortest time. Once your people get over the shock caused by your move, the benefits delivered are immediate. For a start, you get a better feeling for what's going on around your team.

    When you're part of the action, you don't have to waste time working out what's going on. You know instinctively. You overhear stuff. You become part of the conversation. People overhear you. They see you. You're instantly more visible and, most importantly, become more accessible.

    If, from time to time, you need some privacy, leave a little more space around you than the normal workstation. And seat your closest confidants, those who know what's going on in your life, closer to you. I usually have my Executive Assistant and the company CFO nearby. You might need access to a meeting room from time to time, so make sure your desk isn't too far away.

I remind myself **every morning**: **Nothing I say this day** will **teach me anything**. So **if I'm going to learn**, **I must do so by listening**.

Larry King
Broadcaster

This simple, strategic move changes the way in which people view you. Remember, going to the boss's office can be intimidating. The office is a barrier. Sitting in open plan breaks down that barrier and will change the way you interact with your team. In their eyes, you're 'out in the open' and part of the action ready and willing to help when needed.

2. Big Room Meetings

Most organisation structures rely on one group of managers to communicate top-level messages down to the next level of managers who, in turn, deliver it to those at the coalface. Depending on the size of the organisation, this filter process can extend through a few layers. By the time the message reaches its final destination it's been reinterpreted several times. The message that reaches the shop floor or the people who are interacting with your customers will, in all likelihood, bear little resemblance to the original story sent down from the top.

That's why I love big room meetings. You know the sort. The ones where everyone gets together in the big meeting room, the cafeteria or wherever the biggest space is, and you share what's going on. Everyone gets the same message, with the same emphasis and the correct sense of priority. The approach might involve getting some people, those not based in the main office, to connect by phone or video conference to catch the action. In one of my businesses we had the entire 700-person workforce attending the weekly Monday morning meeting. The big room meeting is, in a rapidly changing business, a fantastic way to keep everyone on point and to ensure message consistency to your customers and stakeholders.

Remember, everyone likes to know what's going on. People are fundamentally nosy. And you can tell your people almost everything in business. Be honest, how much is really confidential? Trust your people with information and they'll return the favour tenfold.

3. Morning teas

I was once appointed CEO of a loss-making business with an extremely toxic company culture. Claws came out as the office doors opened each morning and weren't withdrawn until everyone went home at night. Men and women, young and old, each was as bad as the other. Misinformation filled every room and organisational respect was non-existent. Recruitment was almost impossible and our customers regularly received conflicting information.

One of the best things we did to change that culture was to introduce a

Talk to **your people**
about the **things** that
they want to **talk about**.

weekly morning tea. As noted earlier in this chapter, I've done it ever since. Every week, usually on a Wednesday, I'd have morning tea with one of the teams, usually about eight people. It's important to keep the numbers at a level that ensures that those people attending will feel comfortable about contributing. The rules are, as I've already noted above, you bring the muffins and they bring the agenda. In other words, we talk about the stuff that the people, not the boss, want to talk about. The boss can get his or her message out as part of how they respond.

4. **Celebrate successes**

People love to be part of something successful. Remember, in many businesses, the number one thing people worry about is their job security. Celebrating events regularly makes people feel that they are part of something that is successful and it provides a sense of stability. It doesn't have to be a big success and it doesn't have to be a big celebration. It can be a new customer, a big sales deal or even a birthday, a wedding anniversary, or one of your people coaching the local little league team to some success. And it doesn't have to be expensive. A bottle of wine, a dinner for two, or a lunch for the team will often be well received.

And, of course, you will create another opportunity to make a short speech to your team while thanking or congratulating one of their workmates or the group they're all part of. Once again, you are visible, accessible and real. That's what they want you to be.

> *My daughter recently completed her business degree and is in the second year of her dream job at one of the major advertising agencies. She's one of the most junior people in the place and is doing everything she can to learn the advertising business from the bottom up.*
>
> *Recently, she applied for a day's leave to attend her university graduation ceremony. The following day, the Managing Director, Director of Client Services and HR Director of the agency took her out to a nice restaurant for a celebration lunch.*
>
> *How big an impact do you think that has on a young person starting out?*

Simple things, done well, make a big difference.

5. **Friday night drinks (only once a month)**

A word to the wise: don't use this practice to create a booze culture. Done

Block out time in your **diary** to **walk around the floor** and **talk** to your **people**. How difficult can that be? It's not . . . but managers don't do it.

properly, you can provide another opportunity to wander around the team in a relaxed environment and talk about the week or month just gone. In this environment you'll hear about some of the customer issues that might not otherwise filter through to you, or issues around a product's pricing, or maybe the fact that you're having difficulty recruiting a junior role. Sometimes, you'll feel the need to take action and other times you won't. Either way, it's another opportunity for you to listen and your people to see you as an approachable member of the team, rather than the boss.

In today's health and safety-conscious environment there are other things to consider here. Do you have the function on-site or off-site? On-site is better as people are more likely to turn up. Off-site may be better suited to the company's alcohol policy. When setting up, make sure the drinks are only for an hour or so and that people are encouraged to obey drink-drive rules. Remember, it's not about the drinking, it's about the opportunity for two-way communication. If your organisation is serious about caring for its people, making sure they get home safely is the right thing to do and it reinforces your cultural objectives.

Done properly, and safely, it's another great way to interact with your people.

6. **Walk the floor**

I like to diarise time to 'walk the floor' two or three times a week. I do it to be seen, to listen and to learn. I enjoy stopping by a salesperson's workstation to find out how they are getting on. I enjoy chatting to our sales teams or our customer service people in the call centre and hearing what issues they are dealing with each day. It provides a little health check on the business. But you must be disciplined to do it.

Your activity doesn't always have to be planned in one-hour segments. Take a different route through the office as you walk to the kitchen or bathroom — you'll bump into different people along the way. Allow an additional five minutes as you go to a meeting or head for the car park and stop by and check in on one of your people as you go.

Remember, your people want to be led and they want to know that you care about what they are doing. You need to communicate those things as often and as honestly as you can.

Postscript: Communication

My last words of advice on the importance of communication and these simple rules around messaging are as follows:

- Be consistent and stick to the same story.
- Ensure that your people know what they are meant to be doing.
- Keep your messages simple. Simple, straightforward messages are more likely to be accurately communicated and remembered.
- Make sure your own actions are always consistent with the messages you share with your people.
- If something isn't being done properly, make sure that the person responsible knows it's their job, before berating them.
- No matter how busy you are, schedule communication time, to wander, talk to people and visit customers. Be visible. Be accessible.
- Have fun communicating with your people.

* * *

Leadership is **solving problems.**
The day your soldiers **stop bringing you**
their problems is the **day** you have
stopped leading them.
They either have **lost confidence** that
you **can help** or have **concluded** that
you **do not care.**

General Colin Powell
Former Secretary of State
United States of America

'C' word' #3: Consistency

'As the leader, you need to be constantly aware that your actions are being observed by the team. The expectations of your people will reflect the standards you set and the behaviours you accept. In the era of social media, it has never been so important to act in a manner that is consistent with the objectives and aspirations you are seeking to achieve and the resultant expectations that you have of your people.'

Previous generations have lived in class-based societies that enabled — in fact, required — leaders to behave in a manner that was totally different and substantially more privileged than was expected by their people. Think about the old textile factories of the past. Or the military during the two world wars. One rule for the workers or troops. But quite another for the managers and generals.

Over the course of my career, I have noticed more and more how the leaders are expected not to ask anything of their people that they are not prepared to do themselves. It hasn't always been like that. Like a lot of my views on leadership and management, my thinking on this topic developed as a result of an event.

It was a briefing for senior managers at a major global retail company in the mid 2000s. I can't name the company, as I wasn't present. However, the company had been a client of the consulting firm I had worked with and one of my former colleagues was in the room. The business environment at the time was challenging and the retail sector in particular was feeling the pinch.

The highly paid CEO was on the podium talking about the state of the market and how the company had failed to respond to the situation as well as some of their competitors had done. As a result, revenues were down as some had expected, but surprisingly, market share had taken a major hit as well.

The CEO went on to talk about the changes that would be made. Costs would be cut and many people would lose their jobs. New head-count levels would be declared and then frozen until further notice. Overtime would be banned and a number of retail outlets would be closed.

He then encouraged his people to respond to the challenges the organisation faced and asked for extra commitment and effort from everyone to help the company get through the difficult time. As the team shuffled away at the end of the presentation, there was lots of chatter among the managers, most of it understanding and constructive about the job ahead.

Social media means that you are **always visible**. Make sure that you **act in a manner** that is **consistent** with what you **want** your **people** and your **customers to see**.

Then something changed.

Following the session, the CEO and members of the company's board of directors boarded two helicopters and flew to a nearby country club for an afternoon of golf.

Even in the days before Facebook and Snapchat, you can imagine how long it took for this to get around the management team. What do you think this action did to the attitude of the people who had been in the room earlier that day?

Interestingly, the company never recovered, and was subsequently acquired by one of its competitors. The point is this. If you are giving the people the information they need to do their jobs — you are communicating — you then need to be part of the solution. You can't just leave it to them. They need to see that you are committed to the cause more than anyone else in the team. That's where your believability comes from. Your people want to see your commitment to work with them and do whatever it takes for all of you to be successful.

If you think that the lessons from the GFC have stopped this sort of thing from happening, think again.

At the time of writing, at the Australian base of a global company I know well, people are working incredibly hard. The business has had a fantastic run of winning new business. In addition, their clients are increasing the workloads to maximise the opportunity offered by the growing economy. Added to that is the fact that this particular team have lost a couple of key people due to the pressure and they are finding it difficult to recruit capable talent, probably because most of their competitors are enjoying a similar golden run.

As a result, this team comprises people who are working past 10 p.m. most evenings and frequently past midnight. When this happens in any business you will get pressure, tears, tantrums and 'dummy spits'. But properly led, these situations also offer an opportunity to build strength, loyalty and unity in a team. In fact, I believe that you can build a better team during difficult times like these than you can in less stressful times.

Recently, at this particular company, the leader of the business returned to the office at 4.30 p.m., after an unexplained absence of two hours. Asked where he had been. He openly and unashamedly responded that he'd been at the gym and that he 'felt fantastic'.

Can you imagine how his overworked and deeply stressed team felt?

Don't ask the team to **do stuff** you
are **not prepared to do yourself.**
Nothing beats **leading by example.**

To me, this guy just doesn't get it. I'm not saying that, as the leader, you need to be the first to arrive at the office and the last to leave. However, I am saying that you have to be connected to and conscious of what your people are going through. Leaders have to be highly sensitive to the needs of their people. The correct term is empathy. If you don't understand it, look it up. When the pressure is on, you have to show proactive support and compassion to the members of your team.

The leader might have earned the right not to be rowing as hard as everyone else (although I even find that difficult to accept), but he or she has to be in the same boat. I have to say that it frustrates me to see managers getting it so wrong.

There are a number of useful questions that come out of these examples:

1. Does the leader understand what the people are going through?
2. Does he or she understand the impact of their own actions?
3. What can we do to get them to understand the situation?

Firstly, good leaders will create forums for discussion among the team. Think about my earlier notes regarding morning teas and similar opportunities. Create the setting where your people can discuss the challenges of the current environment? In doing so, make sure they feel comfortable about speaking up without the fear of recrimination.

Just creating the opportunity to discuss the situation does a number of things:

- People feel listened to;
- They get to express their frustrations (or get it off their chest, so to speak);
- They get the chance to have the leader hear of their circumstances;
- They develop a hope that you will do something about it (which keeps them going a bit longer);
- They walk away feeling better because 'now he/she knows'.

In recent years there has been plenty of talk about the importance of EQ, as distinct from IQ. This has been particularly noted when recruiting people. It is even more important when looking at the appointment of people for leadership roles. We all understand that IQ (or intelligence quotient) measures intelligence. But despite it being a rather fashionable discussion topic, EQ (or emotional quotient) remains new to many people. EQ measures your emotional intelligence, or, simply, your ability to understand other people and how to work with them. It includes self-awareness, empathy (understanding how other people feel in a given situation) and

How's your **EQ**?

Don't know what it means?

LOOK IT UP.

social skills or people skills (your ability to interact with others).

The two leaders in the examples above may well have high intelligence, and probably outstanding industry expertise, but based on their actions, they would both appear to score low in EQ.

It's one thing to understand what your people are going through. It's another thing altogether to have them know that you understand and that you care. I remember the aforementioned sales superstar Zig Ziglar had a wonderful way of describing this. He said:

> **'People don't care how much you know,**
> **until they know how much you care . . . about them.'**

While Zig was talking about his relationship with customers, there is no doubt in my mind that the same rule applies to your relationship with the people in your team.

The only way your people will really know that you care about them is for you to get around the team and have those informal one-on one conversations. Here are some questions to start the conversation to enable you to check in with the emotional needs of your team.

> *'Hey, I know that there's a lot going on at the moment. How are you coping?'*
> *'I see that you're still here most evenings when I leave the office. What time are you getting out of here at the moment?'*
> *'How is your partner [or the kids] coping with you being here this late?'*
> *'As you know, resourcing is tough at the moment. We're finding it hard to get more people. Is there anything else we can be doing to help you?*

Or how about this as you walk out the door at the end of the day?

> *'How much longer are you likely to be? Don't forget you have a family to get home to.'*

These questions don't necessarily solve the problems in the short term, but they do show that you care and that you are open and willing to have a conversation about the things that people are finding difficult. As the leader, you are seen as being more interested, more appreciative and more approachable as a result.

Consistency means being connected to what your people are going through and

People **don't care how much you know**, until they know **how much you care . . . about them**.

Zig Ziglar
Salesman, speaker, author

putting yourself on the line as much as they are. It means acting in a manner that is absolutely consistent with what you expect of them. If times are tough, head-counts are frozen and bonuses aren't being paid, be cautious about turning up to work in a new car. (I know it sounds basic and obvious, but you would not believe, dear reader, how out of touch many managers become.) Be equally cautious about those Facebook snaps of your holiday in the sunshine while the team is buried back home.

Similarly, if you are having a major restructure of the business and privileges are being lost, make sure that you and your lieutenants are not excluded from the list of sacrifices that have to be made. We often see bosses getting big bonuses while their teams are making cutbacks, and it's a bad look. You might recall the immediate aftermath of the GFC when companies that had been 'bailed out' by various governments spent some of that money on big bonuses for those who, in many cases, had contributed to the collapse. Save the big bonuses for the times when there are big successes and everyone is on the winning side.

When you boil it all down, your people are there to help you to be successful. The best thing that you can do is to help them, enable them and support them. If you can get alongside your people and help them to be the best that they can be, you have the greatest possible chance of succeeding as a leader.

∗ ∗ ∗

Postscript: 'C' words

Here's the full list of my 'C' words — the 13 behaviours of successful leaders.

1. Clarity — Be clear about what you are trying to achieve.
2. Communication — Get the message out. Make sure your people understand what you are trying to achieve.
3. Consistency — Act at all times in a manner that is consistent with what you are trying to achieve and what you are expecting of your people.
4. Care — Develop a genuine interest in and appreciation for your people and your customers.
5. Commitment — Create an unrelenting focus on the objectives, priorities and actions at all times.
6. Change — Constantly review your performance against the dynamics of the market at large and look for opportunities to improve.
7. Challenge — Push yourself. Work with your people to set goals that are 'out of reach but not out of sight'. (Quote: Denis Waitley)
8. Camaraderie — Respect your people. Treat them as colleagues rather than subordinates, inform them, reward them and share the success.
9. Collaboration — Work together towards a shared vision, common understanding and maximising all available resources.
10. Competence — Attention to detail, capability and understanding of the business and industry, capacity for work.
11. Customers — Recognise that without them you don't have a business. Work with them to get their help in developing your business.
12. Courage — To continually challenge the status quo, try new things, and rapid response to new opportunities.
13. Cheerfulness — Because, after all, we spend too much of our lives working, we may as well enjoy it.

I know it's an oldie,
but it's also a goodie . . .
If you are **failing to plan**,
you are **planning to fail**.

CHAPTER 5

The Power of Planning

'Why is there such a persistent gap between ambition and per-formance? . . . Our research reveals that, on average, 95% of a company's employees are unaware of, or do not understand, its strategy. If the employees who are closest to customers and who operate processes that create value are unaware of the strategy, they surely cannot help the organization implement it effectively.'

The Office of Strategy Management
Robert S. Kaplan and David P. Norton
Harvard Business Review, October 2005

Business planning doesn't have to be that hard!

If you don't currently have a business plan, don't worry. You are in the majority. Yes, it's true that most businesses don't have a plan. Their people just go to work each day and deal with whatever comes along. It's called 'reacting'!

In the great majority of cases, plans just fail to materialise — they simply don't get written. Those organisations simply react to what's going on around them every day and are swept along in the process.

In other cases, plans are created, only to be lost in the bowels of a filing cabinet where they remain unsighted until a year or so later when they re-emerge for a brief run as the template for a new edition, one that will in all likelihood meet the same fate. At other times the plan will fail, not because the plans themselves are deficient, but because the leaders whose job it is to implement them lack the managerial stamina or competency to do so properly.

If most of those plans that are developed fail, you might well say 'Well, why

Most **businesses** are **bad at planning** and **execution**.

But **small** to **medium** businesses and **family businesses are the worst!**

Even where plans do exist, **most organisations fail due to poor execution**.

bother?' The answer to that is quite simple. In my experience, the business leaders and managers who do have a very clear view of what they're doing and why are truly successful.

If you can develop a well-targeted business plan that suits the needs of your business, communicate it well to your people and your customers, and maintain a relentless focus on achieving the goals you set for yourself, your chances of being successful will dramatically increase. What's more, you will be more successful than you anticipated.

Despite this, most businesses don't have plans, and of those that do, the majority fail. The reasons for the failure of business plans are as broad and varied as the plans themselves. However, from what I have seen, there are some common threads across those failed plans. They include:

1. The planning process wasn't taken seriously, or given the appropriate level of time and resourcing. This is often the case in a corporate environment where the divisional plan is being done at the request of 'someone upstairs'. Alternatively, in a mid-sized business the same indifferent attitude prevails when the plan is requested by the bankers or a couple of major shareholders, and management treat it as something unimportant.
2. The plan's expectations are unrealistic and unachievable. This usually comes from a 'gung ho' approach to the planning and budgeting in the first place, and results from a lack of good source information or research going into the planning process from the outset.
3. The people responsible for achieving the key objectives and goals set forth in the plan had no input into developing those plans. As a result they are disengaged in regard to the plan's objectives, and regard many of the goals as unachievable.
4. The plan has not been communicated to the people within the organisation. The result of this is that people don't know what the plan is and are unable to deliver against it.
5. Remuneration and bonus structures within the business are not aligned to the deliverables within the plan. In other words, the key objectives within the plan do not relate to the KPIs (key performance indicators) that drive remuneration within the business.

Owners of most small businesses or family businesses put more effort into plannng a fishing trip than they do their business. But it doesn't matter how large or small your business is, your ability to prepare a well thought out and accurately

Planning?

Where do I start?

targeted business plan is vitally important. And yet, most leaders and managers are struggling to make planning a meaningful process, an effective tool and a means by which to deliver successful business outcomes.

A well-constructed and articulated business plan is a road map. It presents a clear picture of where you are trying to head to and what steps you need to take to get to get your organisation to its ultimate, desired destination. It also provides useful checkpoints, or progress markers, along the way.

A good business plan, well communicated, will have a broad audience. Your people, customers, directors, shareholders, bankers — indeed all of your most important stakeholders — need you to have a plan. Because that's how you will do the best job for them, and it's how everyone, yourself included, can monitor progress. But to be successful, the grand plan must be broken down into components that can be communicated and operationally implemented at every level every day.

* * *

There is one other important factor that, in my experience, inhibits the planning process. Many leaders simply don't know where or how to start building or writing a business plan. This chapter has been written and compiled with that very prevalent reality in mind.

Getting started: The most important question you will ever ask

Successful business planning hinges on the key question I raised earlier in this book: 'What are you trying to achieve?' 'Clarity of purpose' is, as I've said several times, central to being able to get your people and other stakeholders supporting you, your initiatives and the outlook you have for the organisation.

Not so long ago, I spent time with the new shareholders of a recently acquired medium-sized business. Having owned the business for a few months, they now understood what they had purchased and some of the issues and opportunities they'd inherited.

They had, unlike some in a similar position, a basic budget and business plan. I sensed, however, that the documents had been prepared in order to satisfy their banker's needs rather than the purpose being to deliver a coherent plan to enable the enterprise to grow and develop. In fact, their plan didn't really offer them the

Most businesses **don't have a plan**. Of the **15% that do, more than 60% fail to communicate that plan** to their people.

information or analysis they needed to run the business better.

Situations like this occur often. Too many business plans are simply a SWOT analysis accompanied by a list of things to do.

People run companies of all sizes without a plan to help them take their business to where they want to go. In most cases, unfortunately, managers don't know where they want to go. In effect, those managers are turning up each day and guessing.

I'm often asked to help organisations to develop their business plans. And I'm not one of the new age consultants who think a plan can fit on one page. But equally, I like to keep it simple. To do that, I ask a lot of questions. The process helps me clearly establish the objectives and the business aspirations of the shareholders and senior executives. Good questions will also highlight where the issues are as well as where the opportunities might lie.

So while I ask many questions, the one that's more important than all the others combined is, as I keep stating: **'So, what are you trying to achieve?'**

I recently asked this question to one of the senior executives in one of Australia's 'big four' banks. He boldly started to answer but he was waffling not long after and I could see that he was struggling. Halfway through his first sentence he stopped, unable to come up with the right words, and said, 'Can I come back to you on that?'

Our reasons for being in a business vary widely, almost to the point of everyone having a different rationale. Consequently, it can often take a lot of time to get everyone clear about what the key objectives are. And that's okay. It's worth taking the time because unanimous agreement about the answers to this question is so important that it will drive many of the other decisions that you'll make in your business.

As it does in so many aspects of leadership, clarity of purpose is the key to creating and implementing a successful planning regime.

As the leader you may be a chief executive who's accountable to a board of directors. At the other end of the scale, you may be a sole proprietor that relies on some help from your accountant. Elsewhere in between you may be running a team in someone else's business. Irrespective of the size of the business, or the nature of your role, as the leader you must provide for your team with clarity around the key things you want to achieve and how that relates to the key priorities within the business.

Being clear about your core purpose and key objectives provides you with a

A **SWOT analysis**
accompanied by a **to-do list**
is **not** a **plan**.

backbone against which to measure your strengths and weaknesses, and ultimately to make decisions. It will help you to define the type of people you need, what new products to stock, or the location of your premises. It will help you to determine what's going well and what's not.

As part of the planning process you should look for areas where the business needs to improve or identify aspects of the business that are being done poorly. Look for opportunities that you're not taking full advantage of, and try to spot risks that might impact your operation in the near future. Leaders must take ownership of the key elements of the plan and lead by example. Clearly show the importance of each issue you're addressing and openly support the initiatives taken to do so.

Every business needs a plan. Every leader needs a plan. You need to develop your own plan. An idea is not a plan and neither is a goal that doesn't specify the actions that need to be taken. A SWOT analysis or a to-do list isn't a plan either. A business plan highlights the key objectives of the organisation over a period of time. Within that plan should be a series of priorities. And each of those priorities should have its own series of project plans.

Of the business plans that do exist, most fail due to poor execution. So your approach to planning has to take that risk of failure away. The process outlined below enables the execution via a series of project plans that are delivered by the people who are best positioned to successfully execute each component of the plan.

Introducing OPIATs

My approach to planning provides a way to keep everyone, particularly the leaders and managers, tuned into the organisation's overall goals. I like to be very specific about each particular operational priority and clearly identify whose job it is to lead and be responsible for each and every action required to deliver the components of the plan.

My preference is therefore to break the process down into the following steps:

1. **Strategic priorities**. What are your main strategic priorities (or headlines)? Ideally you will have between six and 10 of these. Some generic examples might include:
   a. To recruit and retain outstanding people;
   b. To deliver outstanding customer service;
   c. To be a highly innovative organisation, regularly creating new products;
   d. A need to grow sales by X% in the next 12 months;

Make sure that your **planning process involves the people** who will be responsible for helping you to **deliver the outcomes.**

    e. To develop and maintain an outstanding health and safety record; or

    f. To become world class at process compliance.

2. **Issues and opportunities**. Within each strategic priority, you will then develop a list of issues and opportunities that relate to that headline and your need to improve in that area.

3. **Project plans**. For each of the issues or opportunities you have highlighted, you should then develop a project plan. Each project plan will be one to two (maximum) pages long and outline the clear plan that you are going to implement in order to improve your performance in that area.

Your business plan will ultimately comprise a number of project plans that are designed to help you respond to the issues and opportunities within the business. In order for the various components of the plan, or even a project within the plan, to be successful it is important to:

- Involve people at every level in the development of and the execution of the plan. Success will only come if your people are engaged and they will engage if they are part of the decision process up front.

- Ensure that the plan is a living document, one that is constantly referred to. Most plans never make it to a management or team meeting. They are written, presented (maybe), and quickly forgotten. Your goal here is to ensure that the planning document, whatever form it may take, is at the centre of your operational activity and decision-making.

Here's a brief example to get you thinking about strategic priorities and issues and opportunities:

*Let's imagine that one of the key objectives in the business plan is the 'need to dramatically improve our customer experience and the quality of our customer relationships'. This may have been highlighted by a situation where the organisation is experiencing declining customer numbers, or the arrival of a new competitor. As a result this becomes one of your six to 10 **strategic priorities**.*

Within that priority, having conducted a review of the situation, which has probably involved speaking to customers, a review of customer queries or complaints, as well as discussions with a number of people internally, we

What does **OPIAT** mean?

One-page issues and actions template.

*might highlight the following key items as our **issues and opportunities**:*

- *The turnaround times for customer queries;*
- *Accuracy of our billing/invoicing;*
- *Responsiveness to new business enquiries by our sales team;*
- *How customers are greeted in store;*
- *Operations within our call centre; and*
- *After-sales follow-up is non-existent.*

We now know what we are dealing with. By breaking the plan down into projects under each of these items, we would then seek to set up a project plan for each of these key issues and opportunities. As a result, you are able to get the right people working on the areas that you need to improve in a focused and timely manner. A project plan will clearly identify:

- the issue or opportunity;
- what you propose to do about it;
- the individual or group of people who are responsible;
- the timeframes you are working to;
- what the result will look like when the job's finished;
- the schedule of follow-up discussions to check that you're on schedule.

As a result, the plan remains alive, and the people have accountability for achieving it.

Within each project, I like to use a one-page issues and actions template (OPIAT) that I have developed over the years. (Note: I admit that for some projects, getting everything on one page can be tough. It depends on how good your eyesight is and how small the font is. But you should never need more than two pages.) The key headings follow.

1. **STRATEGIC PRIORITY**. What category or headline from the plan does this issue or opportunity relate to?
2. **ISSUES OR OPPORTUNITIES**. Note: This may be one issue or many, that need to be addressesd as part of your action programme. What are the issues, opportunities, challenges or problems that you must overcome in order to enable you to achieve your aspiration in this area?
3. **IMPACTS**. What is the impact of those issues on the business? This step helps

WHO IS RESPONSIBLE?

Most plans fail on that question alone.

you to understand more about each issue and how it is affecting your ability to achieve your objectives and aspirations. For opportunities, the impact refers to the positive outcomes to be gained by successfully pursuing the opportunity. Be as specific as possible, as this helps to define and prioritise the solutions. (This is the point that most planning processes miss.)

4. **DESIRED OUTCOME**. When this problem is solved, what is your desired outcome? What are we trying to achieve? This is the visionary piece. In other words, what does success look like? When this challenge is overcome, how will it appear to your stakeholders, including your people and customers? How will the resolution affect your business?

5. **OBSTACLES**. What are the obstacles or barriers to success that are preventing us from achieving the desired outcome? Obstacles might come in the form of internal factors such as systems, or external factors such as competitive behaviour.

6. **RESPONSIBILITY**. Who is responsible? This is self-explanatory: which member of the team will drive this initiative and who will they get to help them?

7. **COMMUNICATION**. Who are the stakeholders who need to be communicated with? Critical to the success of any project is bringing along the key stakeholders from outside the responsible group, ensuring that they are informed and consulted.

8. **AGREED ACTION PLAN**.
   a. **30-day actions** — what are we going to do in the next 30 days to get this under way? Usually the 30-day action involves getting better data and information about causes of the issue, or alternatively details of the opportunity, and its impact.
   b. **60-day actions** — what are the next series of actions required? As the initial snapshot of the issue or opportunity is developed, it is time to start developing plans to address the challenge. By 60 days, we should be working on solutions and starting to implement.
   c. **90-day actions** — by 90 days we are into execution mode. Focus should be on putting actions in place, which address the issue or pursue the opportunity, as well as dealing with the additional matters that have arisen out of the process to date.

9. **12-MONTH PLAN**. The 12-month outlook becomes the immediate goal we are pursuing. Where do we expect to be with this initiative in 12 months? We need to acknowledge that some plans will be complete within that time, whereas major projects may take longer.

Your **main objective** is that **your plan** remains an **active, living document** that is **referred to regularly**.

I hope you can see that, by using this format for each project, you are provided with a clear picture of what the issue is, how it impacts the business, the targeted activity, the people who are responsible for delivering the outcomes, and the key actions and programmes they will be implementing in doing so.

The one-page issues and actions template ensures that you have a live document that is updated at every monthly meeting, with clear accountability or responsibility, and an agreed plan of activity. As the team leader, each month you simply go through the 30-day actions with your team, check off what's been done and then 'roll the plan' forwards. In other words, as you complete your first 30 days, simply roll the 60- and 90-day actions forward and develop a new list of 90-day actions to work towards. Be sure to capture any uncompleted actions so nothing is lost. Do this every month as the programme develops.

As a result, the plan stays alive. Depending on the size of the organisation you can have anything from 20 to 50 OPIATs, which drive the business improvement programme.

This approach clearly identifies each issue or opportunity and you are now in a position to measure its impact on the business. In doing so, everyone in the leadership team either agrees or disagrees about the severity of the issue, or the magnitude of the opportunity, making it easier to prioritise its importance. The 30-, 60- and 90-day actions become a rolling 90-day plan, which can be used to drive your team meetings and activities programme. Every initiative or challenge can be managed using this relatively simple process. And the name of the person responsible for driving each initiative is there for all to see. As a result, the action emanating from the plan remains current. The planning paper lives with every manager with a responsibility, rather than heading for the filing cabinet.

Let's look at a real example and take it down to the project planning level so you can see how it might look.

Case study

I recently spent some time working with a client that is a major operator in the utilities sector. As part of their planning process, they set a goal to dramatically improve the experiences their customers had when they interacted with the organisation.

There are, of course, many components to the customer experience issue in a large organisation. For the purposes of this illustration I'll focus on just one, the ability to resolve a customer query or complaint when a customer calls into the call centre for the first time. Call centres call this their 'first call resolution rate'.

Step 1:

Understand the issue and the **impact** of the **issue** on the **business.** **Solutions** can come **later.**

This company's first call resolution rate was 15%. In other words, when a customer called their 0800 number and spoke to a call centre operator, the operator was able to solve the problem, or deal with the issue during that call, just 15% of the time! Conversely, there was an 85% chance they wouldn't.

We weren't, at this point, trying to resolve issues such as how long it took to answer the call or any other performance issues relating to the call centre or the 0800 number. We focused only on how to resolve the query quickly and efficiently.

The action plan that emerged from our thinking looked like this:

1. STRATEGIC PRIORITY: To deliver an outstanding customer experience.

2. ISSUE OR OPPORTUNITY

Customer experience in the call centre is not good enough. Customer calls to the 0800 number result in slow responses, unresolved queries and we are frequently presented with inaccurate information resulting in an inability to resolve the issues.

3. IMPACTS

85% of customer calls are unresolved on the first call. Consequently, customer satisfaction is poor and frustration is high. When an unresolved call is completed, execution in resolving the issue offline and getting back to the customer is poor, with our response often taking more than four weeks. As a result there is a backlog of more than 5000 customer queries and complaints.

Additional business costs include a team of people working on the backlog offline. These people must re-familiarise themselves with the problem, sometimes re-calling the customer to assist their understanding of the initial query. Customer frustration remains high over the course of the process — which sometimes takes up to six months to resolve. In some cases, the company does not even get back to the customer, whom must then call again and recommence the process.

4. DESIRED OUTCOME

Improve our first call resolution rate as per the following targets:
- 50% by the end of year 1
- 70% by the end of year 2
- 85% by the end of year 3

Reduce backlog from current average of three months to two weeks by the end of the first year. Our ultimate goal is to have 90% of all calls resolved during the first call. Those that aren't will ultimately be resolved within 72 hours.

This is the time to be **honest with yourself** about the **obstacles** that are **really present**. Too many people make **excuses** in order to **avoid the real issues**. Don't imagine stuff that isn't there or doesn't matter.

5. OBSTACLES
- Lack of key technology including call centre scheduling software, and call centre personnel access to customer invoice details and works requests.
- A number of call centre personnel have been in place for a long time and are wedded to old processes. Personnel review (including team leaders) will need to be cautiously managed and the Union informed.

6. PERSON RESPONSIBLE
Project team to be led by Simon Johnson [name changed]. Simon will co-opt two people from complaints team (Sally and Jenson) as required.

7. COMMUNICATION PLAN
Monthly updates to the sales team, call centre team, reception, CEO and exec team. First communication to go out from the CEO during the first 30 days announcing the project, who's leading it, and key objectives.

8. AGREED ACTION PLAN
30 days
- Analysis of inbound calls to understand the content of the queries and complaints. For example, how many related to invoicing, installation times, or technical callouts?
- Commence communication process as above.
- Commence review of technology and processes.

60 days
- Completion of technology review.
- Identification of the top three causes of customer calls in the first instance, and the development of a plan to address each issue so, where possible, the call centre operator can respond while online.
- Correct technology issues identified as they relate to top three causes.
- Commence personnel assessment.
- Review training processes and begin skills review.

90 days
- Commence implementation of resolutions within the call centre team, starting with easy-to-execute solutions with high initial payoff.
- Develop plan for improved training of call centre operators to ensure that changes are supported.
- Commence analysis of alternative technology solutions, including additional software for call centre workstations.

The world is moving **so fast**,
that **30-, 60-** and **90-day plans**
are **essential** to your ability
to **manage change**,
challenges and **chance**.

- Review progress to date and develop action plan for the next three priority causes.

9. 12-MONTH POSITION

Goal is to have 50% of all calls to the 0800 call centre resolved during the first call at the end of 12 months. We will institute an ongoing activity programme to continuously improve performance and to enable achievement of the 24-month goal of 70%. Achieve backlog reduction targets as per the desired outcome above.

* * *

I hope you can see the simplicity of this experience. Note that you don't need to have a lot of action items for each 30-day period, because you are constantly updating the required actions as you progress. Note also that the early focus is on understanding the problem, rather than leaping to solutions. The solutions will come in due course.

In this particular case, as it turned out, 38% of the company's queries and complaints related to the customer's invoice. By adding a billing software program to the call centre computer terminals and by training call centre operators on how to read the accounts and interpret client invoices, the company quickly resolved almost all invoicing complaints during the initial call.

I have now been using the OPIAT approach for many years, with some outstanding results. At a large Australian media company, for example, we identified 51 main issues and opportunities facing the company. Using these one-page issues and actions project-planning templates, we developed a one-page plan to tackle each issue or opportunity. The plan identified the issue, its impact on the business, identified whose job it was to action the plan, and then outlined what would be done in the next 30, 60 and 90 days. The results achieved were rapid and outstandingly successful.

When I was the CEO at Yellow Pages NZ, our entire plan consisted of 45 OPIATs. Each of the one-pagers sat under one of our nine strategic planks or priorities. Those priorities consisted of things like 'attracting, retaining and developing high-quality people' (because we had a major recruitment issue when I arrived there) or 'creating outstanding customer experiences' (to focus on our poor customer service record). We had also identified the need for 'enabling our systems' and the creation of 'a high-performing sales organisation'. So under each strategic priority, such as people, sales, systems or customers, we had between four and six key initiatives — each of them with their own OPIAT, each with a person responsible and each with very specific things that were to be done over the next 30, 60 and 90 days.

If you **tell your friends** that you want to **run a marathon**, you are more likely to **train well** and **complete the goal**. Business plans are **no different**. **Tell your people** about your **plan**, and you will be **more likely** to **achieve** the outcomes.

This approach to planning allows you to attach your main business goals to the key priorities that need to be addressed, thus providing a mechanism for you to reach those goals. Using the 30-, 60- and 90-day plans as a rolling activity schedule, you can manage the action plan as part of your organisation's daily activity. The actions required by the business plan don't need to be separated from the other day-to-day stuff you're trying to do and instead become complementary.

And, don't forget to tell your people what you are doing.

* * *

Communicating the plan

With the planning pages in place, you now need to keep focused on seeing the plan through. Stay true to your key objectives. Constantly ask whether your priorities and plans address your objectives. Most organisations that get the planning process under way, and sometimes even those that complete the plan, become distracted by day-to-day events and the plan 'fizzles out'.

It matters little how good your plan is if it's not implemented.

A lack of confidence can become the issue. Leaders and managers sometimes know where they want to go and even have an idea about how to get there. But then they lack the confidence to tell their people to 'put the blinkers on' and go for it. Why? I can only guess that fear of failure plays a role.

So you have to commit to communicating your plan. It's like any series of goals. Once you tell people, you are more committed to the change programme. Often, management will develop a plan but fail to communicate it to their people and other key stakeholders. You must, as part of your planning, think about and plan the communications process that goes with it.

The key messages that you need to get out to your people include:

- The core components of the plan, including organisational priorities, key actions required to achieve them, and an aspirational vision of what success looks like.
- Specific activity, people responsible and timeframes, so your people understand why some of their colleagues are getting involved in the projects, and what is expected of them, their divisional managers and their colleagues;
- How people are expected to contribute to realising the objectives within the plan. In other words, how individual behaviours and actions must change to achieve the key objectives.

It doesn't **happen** . . .
unless it's **someone's job**.

Keep it simple. Leaders must get out of their offices and communicate the following face to face:

- what you're doing;
- why you're doing it;
- how the changes will affect people's roles;
- how the teams and individual team members can contribute to your various planning projects;
- timeframes and expectations.

As another side benefit, a well-communicated plan publicly binds the leaders and managers to the objectives or priorities, meaning that your people will expect follow-up and action.

* * *

Accountability

As I have tried to stress above. The accountability around your plan must be specific. Plans are often insufficiently specific and organisations fall at the 'how to' hurdle. As you can see in the example above, key actions must be outlined, responsible people nominated and timeframes identified. It helps to break the issues or opportunities down into the steps that need to be taken and the things that need to be done.

Make your people accountable in regular meetings or follow-up sessions to ensure that people are coping, that actions are happening and the plan is being implemented. Remember, nothing happens unless the job is assigned to someone. It's all very well having priorities and goals, but whose job is it to lead each initiative?

Members of your team must be clear about who's responsible for leading each initiative. And people must be given the authority and ability to get on with the job. By the way, don't leave it to the CEO or team leader to lead each initiative. This is a major opportunity to get your people involved and engaged. In fact, ideally, it's better if the CEO is just the conductor, the front person making the announcements to show that he or she is supportive of the process, and the public advocate for the elements of the plan.

Postscript 1: Sample planning process

Struggling to get under way? Here is a step-by-step series of questions, activities, conversation starters and ideas to assist you in developing your business plan. These notes are intended as a guide only and are not intended to be completely exhaustive. You don't have to cover everything on this list, and you are welcome to add to it to suit your type of business.

You will note that I like to ask lots of questions before the real planning starts. The questions and comments are designed to get a conversation going within your team and to get your people involved and engaged in the process. Follow this process to help you to identify your strategic priorities and the issues and opportunities that exist across the business.

1. Clarity of purpose

Jim Collins, in his excellent book *Good to Great* called it the BHAG, or Big Hairy Audacious Goal. Others call it your core purpose, or in my case I simply say 'What are you trying to achieve?' Here you are setting yourself a challenging long-term goal, which is measurable, easy to communicate and understand, and consistent with how you behave. Note, ideally your BHAG must be inspirational and overwhelmingly difficult to achieve!

2. Vision

- What does your business look like in five years?
- What are your forward-looking goals and aspirations?

3. Mission

- What are we trying to achieve and why?
- How would you describe the organisation's core purpose, its goals and aspirations?
- Include what type of organisation you want to be part of.

4. Values

- How do we behave?
- How do we treat our people, our customers and our shareholders?
- What type of organisation do we want to be?
- Common words include honesty, integrity, equality, excellence, service, respectful, etc.

Greatness is not a **function**
of **circumstance**.
Greatness, it turns out,
is largely a matter of **conscious choice**,
and **discipline**.

Jim Collins
Author
Good to Great and
Built to Last

5. Current status

What is the current status of the business? Form a view on performance in regards to current revenues, profitability, people numbers, locations, customer expectations versus delivery, and market position. Identify areas that are going well and other aspects that are not as good as they could be. I like to give each option a score out of 10. For example, revenues are 9/10, but profitability is only 6/10. Immediately you can see an issue.

6. Capability

- What are we really good at?
- What are we not particularly good at?
- What do our customers like about us?
- What do our customers dislike about us?
- How do our people feel about us?
- Do we regularly achieve our targets?
- Are we as good as, or better than, our competitors?
- How do we rate our performance in regard to achievement of financial targets?

7. 80/20 rule

- Does the 80/20 rule apply to our business?
- If so, what parts of the business generate 80% of the outcomes?
- Do the parts of the business that generate the remaining 20% serve a purpose?
- Does this exercise highlight things that you shouldn't be doing, or other things that you should be doing more of?

8. Profitability

- Are we as profitable as we should be?
- If not, why not? Do we have a revenue problem, a costs problem or both?
- Do our people understand how their business unit contributes to profit performance?
- Are we tolerating loss-making parts of our business for strategic reasons? If so, can we justify why we are doing that, and are those strategic reasons still relevant?
- Do we have parts of our business that are not strategic or profitable? If so, why are we continuing with that activity?

9. Positioning

- Does our business model work for us?

Ask lots of good **questions**:
What is the current **status** of your
business?

What are you doing **really well?**

What are you doing **very poorly?**

Are your people **good enough?**

What do your **customers think of you?**

Don't know the answers? Get out, **talk
to people** and **find out**.

- Are we high price, low volume, narrow market, high value add? OR
- Are we low price, high volume, broad market, low value add?
- Are we neither? In that case, what are we? Does our position work in the market that we are active in?

10. Competition
- How many major competitors do we have?
- Who are they and how would you rank them?
- Where do we rank alongside them?
- In each case, where are they better than us?
- In each case, where are we better than them?
- What can we do better to respond?
- Do our competitors offer products or services that we don't, but should?
- Do any of our competitors provide us with an acquisition opportunity?

11. New competitors
- Are there potential new entrants?
- Do we know who they are?
- What are the potential barriers to new entrants?
- Are there smarter ways to do what we do?
- If we were starting again, would we do it the same way?
- Is there a technology solution that enables a new competitor to overtake us?
- If we were starting in competition with ourselves, what would we do?

12. Customers
- Who is our target market — now and in the future? (Include geographical, product type and client type.)
- Who are our current customers?
- Who are our competitors' current customers?
- What additional services do they want?
- Is the customer of the future different to today?
- If we could do one additional high payoff activity for our existing customers, what would it be?

13. External factors (Dr Philip Kotler)
External factors include the economic, physical, technological, social, demographic and political environments. There are a number of these that affect every business.

Uber and Airbnb now dominate the global taxi and accommodation industries respectively. Ten years ago, they didn't exist.

What impact will driverless vehicles, electric vehicles, drones, permanent cameras, solar energy and long-life batteries, changes in computing power, improvements in waste management and water management, agricultural developments, improvements in science, medical miracles, ageing population, or communication technologies ...

have on your business in the next five years?

For example:

- Are there social trends (e.g. ageing population) that have a positive or negative impact on us?
- How would a change of government affect our business?
- How would a change in personnel at our bank alter our operational activity?
- Does the growing role of social media present an opportunity or a risk to our business?
- Is there a tech solution out there that could make us redundant?

14. People

- Describe the current status of our team.
- Are our people good enough?
- Do we have the desired skills and capabilities?
- If not, can we get them?
- Do we have personnel weaknesses in mission critical areas?
- If so, can we move these people elsewhere?
- If not, is this a limiting factor in our plan?
- How consistent is our service delivery? (Give particular attention to same client/ cross border delivery.)
- Do our people behave in a manner that is consistent with our mission and values?
- How are our people paid?
- Does incentive-based remuneration align with our business goals and targets?

15. SWOT (OTSW) = ORCS

By now, you are starting to build up an information base that informs the next phase of the planning process, the SWOT analysis. Note, SWOT analyses are usually carried out in that order: strengths, followed by weaknesses, then opportunities and threats. I prefer to change the order. Consider the opportunities in the market, and any potential threats first. That will make your consideration of strengths and weaknesses more relevant, and better targeted relative to the market opportunity. But OTSW can't be made into a pronounceable word, so I have changed the terminology to suit. ORCS stands for Opportunities, Risks, Capability and Shortfalls. The ORCS analysis is designed to pinpoint where the priorities are relative to what is going on in the marketplace and the environment at large. After choosing the highest priorities, you are then in a position to go to the one-page project plan format. So think about the following two rules for preparing your ORCS analysis:

Discuss **external opportunities** and **risks** before your own **internal capabilities** and **shortfalls**. **External factors** define the **playing field**.

- Consider opportunities and risks before analysing your own capability and shortfalls.
- Be specific. For example, don't just say 'We are weak on the quality of our financial information.' Describe where you are weak, why and later, how you can fix it.

16. Opportunities

Opportunities are favourable factors, which create potential opportunities for you to be successful. They are external to our business or outside our control.

Examples include: A growing market for our products, or a supplier product providing a renewed point of difference.

17. Risks (previously known as Threats)

Risks are unfavourable factors or events, which may lead to deteriorating revenues or profit performance. Risks are also typically external to our business or outside our control.

Examples include: The launch of a major competitor, or an international acquisition resulting in the loss of a major client.

18. Capability (previously known as Strengths)

Our capabilities are things that we do extraordinarily well. They are internal to our business and within our control.

Examples include: Winning new business, or having an extensive store network.

19. Shortfalls (previously known as Weaknesses)

Shortfalls are things that we do poorly. They are typified by issues that are important to our success, but that we are not particularly good at. Shortfalls are internal to our business or within our control.

Examples include: Recruiting the right people, or inadequate systems.

20. Post ORCS — yellow stickies

As you go through the ORCS analysis, write the various opportunities, risks, capabilities, and shortfalls that you have identified from the exercise on yellow stickies. Place the stickies on a whiteboard with a two-by-two grid as on the following page:

We are all **guilty of reacting** to the **urgent** in favour of the **important**. Think about the **ringing phone** that becomes a **pointless call**.

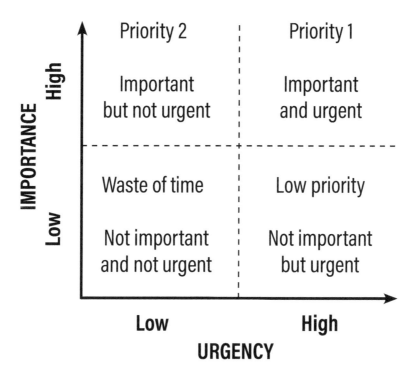

Make sure that you and your team enjoy a good debate about the importance of each issue, and try to gain agreement as to which box that yellow sticky belongs in. Then place each sticky on the importance/urgency chart.

21. The top 20
Identify the top priority issues and opportunities under each heading. (Ideal numbers are in brackets, but don't limit yourself if you feel there are others that are important.)
- Important/Urgent (top 8–10 issues)
- Important/Not Urgent (top 4–6 issues)
- Not Important/Urgent (top 4–6 issues)
- Not Important/Not Urgent (none)

22. Priorities (Part 1)
Identify your top priorities. Give top priority to the issues listed in the top right-hand corner of the grid — the important and urgent. Second priority is given to those items that are deemed important but not urgent. Be sure to focus on areas of major impact only — issues and opportunities that will have at least a 10% impact (positive or negative) on your business.

Priorities: What are the things that can make a **10% difference** to my **business**?

23. Priorities (Part 2)

Narrow lists to 5–6 priorities per category. For categories I like to use the 7 Principles of Profit as a guide. That is, you can categorise under the headings of change, leadership, finance/back office, product or service, sales and marketing, people, and customers. Feel free to categorise in a different way if it suits your business better. For example health and safety (people), innovation (change), sustainability (product and service), social media (marketing) may be more appropriate headlines for your business. Don't throw out those stickies that didn't make the top priorities. Put these 'leftovers' to one side and you can revisit those later. Go through each of the priorities, restate them to a common language and rank them in order of importance.

These 25–40 priorities become your 'Issues and Opportunities'.

24. Review the 'leftovers'

Go back through the yellow stickies that didn't make the list of 'Issues and Opportunities'. Now that you have a complete view of the most important items, there is a chance that you will deem some of these items as a higher priority. Be disciplined. Allow yourself up to only 3–5 additional items.

25. You are now ready to develop the plan

You are now ready to identify your strategic priorities and your list of issues and actions. Your plan will consist of a series of OPIATs (one-page issues and actions templates) developed for each of the identified issues and opportunities. Try to focus on developing more information about each issue to enable you to better define it and understand how it impacts the business.

* * *

The following pages show examples of how the one-page issues and actions planning template looks in practice. Postscript 2 relates to improving the customer experience, while Postscript 3 refers to the very topical area of health and safety.

Postscript 2: OPIAT — Customer Experience

Issues and opportunities project planning template

Strategic priority area: *Improved customer experience*

Define the issue or opportunity.
We are not close enough to our most important customers and lack visibility of their needs and expectations.

What is the impact of this issue/opportunity on the business?
As a result, our customers are looking for alternatives and we are losing business without even knowing it. We are having to discount to 'save' clients.

What is the desired outcome? (That is, what does success look like in the future?)
We are closer to our customers, understand their requirements and adapt to their needs as required. There is no chance they would ever make a decision to change suppliers without our knowledge.

What are the obstacles to achieving the desired outcome?
Our current sales and service teams are not sufficiently focused on our customers, particularly post sale. We are questioning the capability of our talent. In addition, one of our competitors in particular is doing a better job at this than we are.

Who is responsible for leading this? Who will support them?
John Smith — assisted by Sally James and Murray Boyd.

Who are the stakeholders who need to be communicated with?
Sales team, call centre team, reception, CEO and exec team.

Action
- **30 day — what do we need to do in the next 30 days?**
Identify our top 20 customers. Meet face to face with five of them and get their views on our performance. Develop summary snapshot of issues.
- **60 day — what do we need to do in the next 60 days?**
Continue face-to-face discussions with the remaining 15 customers. Shortlist five most common complaints and develop immediate response.
- **90 day — what do we need to do in the next 90 days?**
Client roundtable discussion hosted in the offices, where we present back the outcomes from the face-to-face meetings to our customers and share our proposed solutions.
- **12 months — what do we need to do in the next 12 months?**
Our top 20 clients are reviewed with a member of the management team every quarter and the top 100 receive face-to-face reviews annually.

   We run regular customer roundtables to share our plans and get customer input into new product ideas.

NOTE: 30-, 60- and 90-day plans constantly roll up every month and new 90-day objectives are developed at every checkpoint.

Postscript 3: OPIAT — Health and Safety

Issues and opportunities project planning template

Strategic priority area: *Excellence in health and safety*

Define the issue or opportunity.
H&S procedures are well documented but are not implemented effectively. We appear to have trouble getting the right behaviours in our warehouses and depots. Our drivers can be careless. A major cultural issue.

What is the impact of this issue/opportunity on the business?
We have a high incidence of small accidents and occasional large ones. Workplace injuries are high for our type of business, lost time injuries are expensive and insurance premiums have increased. Some clients have expressed concerns about the lax approach to H&S by our people when on their premises. Worst case, someone gets badly injured or killed.

What is the desired outcome? (That is, what does success look like in the future?)
Our ultimate goal is zero workplace incidents. Short term we should aim for zero lost time injuries. Ideally, our customers will become advocates re H&S.

What are the obstacles to achieving the desired outcome?
The main obstacle is the attitude of our people. H&S is not currently a sufficiently high priority. We need to change attitudes at every level of the company.

Who is responsible for leading this? Who will support them?
Bronwyn (HR Manager) — assisted by Sam (Operations Manager).

Who are the stakeholders who need to be communicated with?
Team leaders, warehouse managers, drivers, storemen, MD

Action
• **30 day — what do we need to do in the next 30 days?**
Set up review of H&S procedures. Review H&S training processes. Conduct initial testing with personnel to understand awareness. Consider appointment of third party to conduct review.
• **60 day — what do we need to do in the next 60 days?**
Discussions with customers — look for examples of inappropriate on-site behaviour. Develop summary snapshot of issues from internal review and customer feedback.
• **90 day — what do we need to do in the next 90 days?**
Presentation of findings to management meeting. H&S improvement plan to be developed, finalised and agreed. Implementation commences.
• **12 months — what do we need to do in the next 12 months?**
Our new training and processes are in place and all existing personnel retrained. All incidents are monitored and followed up with causes identified and corrective action taken. Monthly H&S reporting to management team and board. Twelve-month goal of incidents and injuries halved.

NOTE: 30-, 60- and 90-day plans constantly roll up every month and new 90-day objectives are developed at every checkpoint.

Our **culture** is **friendly** but **intense**.
But if **push comes to shove**,
we'll settle for **intense**.

Jeff Bezos
Founder
Amazon

CHAPTER 6

Culture, Standards and Values

'Quality means doing the right thing when no one is watching.'
Henry Ford
Founder, Ford Motor Company

The old carmaker had it right. A strong culture will take over when there is no one there to give instructions or people aren't sure what to do.

'So, what does culture mean?'

I get asked this question a lot. In fact, there seems to be a lot of talk about culture nowadays. Most of the time we hear it when people are discussing the performance of sports teams.

But just as sports teams can develop a winning culture, so too can teams in business.

Culture is essentially the character of the organisation and it reflects in the way you and your colleagues behave. Culture is represented by a series of values, standards, beliefs and assumptions that drive the behaviour of the people within the organisation and therefore the organisation itself. It is a function of history, hierarchies, structures, aspirations and attitudes. It is often embodied in the knowledge and experience of the enterprise as a whole and those who make that enterprise what it is.

We often refer to the character of a person. We judge people's character by referring to their reputation, their values, and how they treat others. We might form a view on their ethics or morality, or perhaps their integrity. Those views all comprise our opinion of a person's character. Culture refers to the character of the organisation. It's about the environment that your people work in. Not just their

Culture

is represented by a **series of values**, **standards**, **beliefs** and **assumptions** that drive the **behaviour** of the **people** within the organisation.

physical environment, but the attitudinal one, the expectations, the empowerment, and motivation.

As the leader, you are responsible for setting and supporting the tone, the behaviours and the culture within the team or the organisation. You are the culture carrier. If you constantly arrive late, your people will think it's acceptable to be late. If you dress poorly, or swear a lot, your organisation will be scruffy or foul-mouthed. As the culture carrier, you are in charge of how your team looks, behaves and responds.

While it takes time to permanently change cultures within organisations, the arrival of a new leader, or the emergence of an existing one, can create the opportunity to bring incremental changes quite quickly.

If you're running any business, be it extremely large or very small, that business will have a culture that your leadership can influence. More challenging is the position of those of you who lead a team or a division within a larger organisation. You could be forgiven for adopting the position that the organisation culture is set by the management team above, and thus is out of your control. However, you can still influence the culture within your team and I urge you to consider how you might do so.

How your team behaves towards each other, how they respond to a customer, indeed how they conduct themselves, can be influenced by the leadership you provide.

Culture is a difficult thing to understand and is even more difficult to define. It is often more problematic to ascertain the culture of an organisation when you work within it every day, than it is for someone who is looking in from the outside. But if you look very carefully and are prepared to be openly critical, then you will see what you and your team have become.

As I move around different companies, I see numerous cultures. Most of them are weak cultures that support poor performance. We have all heard of 'blame culture' where people fail to take responsibility, and instead point to a colleague or a supplier to highlight what has gone wrong. Or lateness cultures where nothing happens on time. You know the type: you get to the 10 a.m. meeting, only to have the leader of the meeting arrive at 10.10 and the meeting start at 10.15.

I see businesses that have a culture of conflict. They are always fighting with each other. Arguing over what's important, or alternatively the best way to do things. They don't think clients see that. But your customers are not stupid. They see the conflict when one person from your team shares a comment or an opinion and another person's version contradicts that. Other companies have a culture of complaint, where everyone is unhappy.

Company **cultures** are often

NEGATIVE.

There are **businesses** where **nothing**

happens on time.

Meetings start **late.**

People are **slack.**

And deadlines are repeatedly **missed.**

Or we see businesses where poor performance is accepted and underperforming individuals are seldom brought to account. As a result, underperformance is deemed acceptable and becomes the norm.

At the other extreme I see happy organisations, with high levels of social interaction and enjoyment among the team and people who do a really good job. Or I recognise 'can-do cultures' where innovation is strong and energy levels are high. I have also witnessed, particularly recently, very serious organisation cultures that do outstanding work; for example high-end medical practices, where, quite rightly, the focus is on delivering outstanding clinical outcomes.

In fact, the outside observer doesn't have to hang around an organisation for long to start to understand the culture of the place.

If you are an existing leader and you have been in your position for some time, it might be worthwhile revisiting what your team culture really looks like, and what it says about you and your colleagues. If you are new to your leadership role, chances are that you have already formed a view of what the current culture entails and what needs to change.

But you might need to keep the following in mind. Changing a culture for the better is a challenging process. You have existing processes, people and ways of dealing with things that will be ingrained in the organisation and as a result will take a lot of effort to change. And here's the most important point. Setting out to change the culture won't work. As leader you should not set out to fix the culture. You have to set out to change what's wrong with the business. Get the business doing the right things and the culture will follow.

The culture that evolves on your watch will ultimately reflect your own behaviours, the characteristics you personally demonstrate and the way you lead. Having been on both the inside and outside of various businesses as they have undergone dramatic cultural change, I believe that culture is a function of three components. I describe those components as follows:

$$C = L + S + V$$

where

      C = Culture
      L = Leadership
      S = Standards
      V = Values

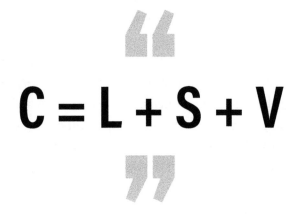

$$C = L + S + V$$

In other words, the organisation's culture will reflect the quality and consistency of the leadership, the standards that the organisation aspires to, and the way the people behave towards each other, their customers and in public.

Leadership drives culture

Leadership reflects the many things we are discussing in this book: clarity of purpose, planning, communication, personnel engagement, consistency, among others. I'm sure that, like me, you've often heard the advice that an organisation needs to change its culture. In my experience, the change in a company's culture is an outcome of actions taken by leaders. It is not an input. Culture is an output. A reflection of behaviours. Doing the right things alongside your people and customers leads to cultural change. Good leaders don't go into a business with a view that they can simply set the desired company culture and have everyone follow along.

Culture change takes time. In my experience, you need a couple of years to change the culture of even a mid-sized organisation. That's the sort of timeframe it takes to develop your plan, get the right people in place, communicate the objectives to your people, and to start making changes that will have a long-term impact on behaviours. Once your people begin to see outcomes of what it is you're trying to do, a change in culture will evolve alongside your transformation programme.

I often talk about some of the actions we took to improve the customer experience at Yellow Pages. After its life as a division of Telecom New Zealand, we inherited an organisation culture that was built on a traditional, old-style, monopolistic business. The Yellow Pages division had originally been a subsidiary of a state monopoly, with no real competitors. It was quite unlike Telecom's core telecommunications business that, by the year 2000, was battling to keep both Vodafone and Telstra at bay in the New Zealand market.

I joined the company as CEO approximately 18 months after it had been sold to a private equity consortium. While the business was still highly profitable, the new wave of competition brought about by Google and others meant that it needed to be much more responsive to the needs of customers.

You will no doubt recognise the characteristics of the old-style monopolistic business structure of the former state sector organisation. Believe it or not, these organisations still exist. Like other businesses with similar backgrounds, the Yellow Pages culture that we inherited exhibited many of the following characteristics:

- a top-heavy management structure;

Culture change is an **outcome**,
not an **input**.
You **don't go into** the **business** seeking to
change the culture.
You **change** the **business**.
The **culture change** will **follow**.

- a bureaucratic approach to doing business;
- taking too long to get things done;
- an organisational structure that included too many people in roles that don't impact the customer;
- a tendency to spend too much time doing business with itself — lots of people holding lots of meetings to discuss internal issues that seldom resulted in a significant impact on the performance of the enterprise;
- a slow response to customer queries and complaints;
- slow internal leadership responsiveness that made people working within the business feel unappreciated;
- insufficient internal and external communication to enable key stakeholders to buy into the objectives of the organisation.

Despite the obvious need for it, in developing our new business plan, I was very conscious not to focus on trying to change that culture. Rather, we focused on a number of key areas, which, if transformed, would lead to a dramatic change to the culture of the organisation.

Here's a brief example.

One of those key high-priority areas was that we set out to 'provide an outstanding customer experience'. We set this objective against an environment where we had daily complaints coming in from customers. Many of those complaints came directly to me. Here are a few quotes from some of that correspondence:

'Your level of customer service is disgusting.'
Steel industry, Christchurch

'I am not happy with the lack of response I have received, and wish to inform you of your general poor service.'
Fruitgrower, Auckland

'For me, dealing with Yellow has been a painful and unpleasant experience.'
Print company, Auckland

Needless to say, this sort of stuff gets your attention. I was getting between five and eight of these letters or emails, sent to me personally, every day. Even though I was new in the hot seat, it didn't take long to realise that we had a problem.

Now that we've taken the **company out of Telecom**, we need to take the **Telecom out of the company**.

*My often-repeated mantra
to the management team
at Yellow Pages*

As a result of this type of feedback, we moved ahead with our customer experience projects in a manner that was all-encompassing for many of our people. Simply put, we had to. Key characteristics of our various activities included the following:

1. **Priority**. We made the provision of an 'outstanding customer experience' one of our nine main strategic priorities.
2. **Seek first to understand**. We spent a lot of time understanding what was leading to the customer complaints and getting to grips with what was going wrong. We then identified the issues that needed to be addressed.
3. **Planning**. We developed a plan of action across the priority areas, with key roles identified, people responsible, and very clear 30-, 60- and 90-day plans for every initiative. These became part of our business plan and monthly management reporting cycle.
4. **People**. We communicated the problem, its impact, our plan, responsibilities and actions to all of our people. Those who were in a position to contribute to the solution were advised on how their role was important to our process. Those who needed additional tools, such as software, to enable them to be more responsive to their clients, received that software and the training to go with it.
5. **Leadership from the top**. The entire initiative was announced by the CEO (me) and supported by me throughout. The Project Leader was the HR Director, because she was in the best place to influence the behaviours of our people.

The outcomes were outstanding. Within 12 months we had delivered the following:

- Our overall customer service level went from 61% to 95%;
- Our first call resolution in the call centre moved from 8.24% to 90.7%;
- Average dispute resolution was reduced from 90-plus days to 72 hours.

Over time the behaviours became automatic, the complaints slowed dramatically, and the people within the business developed a totally different attitude towards the customer. We had changed the culture. But we did so not by focusing on the culture, but by focusing on the issues affecting our performance. Culture change occurred as a result of what we did differently.

* * *

One of the most **important things** for any **leader** is to **never let anyone else define who you are.** And **you define** who **you are.** **I never think of myself** as being the **first woman CEO** of this **company.** I think of myself as a **steward** of a **great institution.**

Ginni Rometty
Chairman, President and CEO
IBM

The 'culture carrier'

Embark on a culture change programme and you must recognise that you're putting your hand up and taking responsibility both for the programme and for its potential outcomes. Culture change is emphatically leadership driven. It is driven from the top. Someone once called the leader of a business the 'culture carrier'. And that is absolutely true. As the leader, you're the person whom your team will look to when they're trying to understand what is expected in the new cultural environment that you're seeking to establish.

I refer you back to the story in the 'Consistency' section where I referred to the global retail company. That is a classic example of the 'culture carrier' getting it very wrong. Whether you like it or not, the organisation's culture will eventually reflect the way you behave.

Thankfully, I've usually been surrounded by highly supportive teams or people who have helped to deliver the business change programmes I've been involved with. Interestingly, in many cases, I inherited terrific teams of people who had seen and recognised the cultural problems, and felt the frustrations long before my arrival, but who had been unable to do anything about the issues because the leadership support wasn't there. They weren't incapable; to the contrary they were outstanding in most cases. Sometimes their talent, or their ability to get things done, was suppressed by my predecessors. Alternatively, a combination of a lack of appropriately targeted leadership, and the fact that the people were overwhelmed by the many issues going on around them and by the need to keep the business running, meant that nobody had the time to stand back and take a good hard look at what was really going on.

Whether you're the CEO, a senior manager, a team leader or a sole proprietor, coming into a business with fresh eyes enables you to see the problems more clearly. I often ask people the following question:

How many pot plants are in the lobby?

Usually, they fail to answer correctly. The point is that everyone walks through the lobby every day, but they don't notice what's there. It's the same with the business in general. The longer you are there, the less likely you are to see the obvious things that need to be fixed.

If you can join a business, see many of the issues quickly, and express a desire to do things to improve the responsiveness of the organisational culture, it will, believe me, be music to the ears of many of your key people. You should try to respond to cultural issues as soon as you see them. The good thing about coming into a

The **leader** of any **organisation** or **team** is the **chief culture carrier**. People **will act** based on what **you imply is important**.

new role is that you have permission to improve things. Your people will, in my experience, quickly jump on board and enthusiastically help you to progress your plans more rapidly than you had imagined.

Despite their support, you will still need to lead the big projects and do so in a hands-on manner. You can't simply come up with an idea, find some willing volunteers to implement it, and then turn your attention to something else. You have to stay with it, attend the progress meetings, keep the momentum going, and keep the new ideas coming. You need to be the cheerleader. Keep walking the talk.

As chief culture carrier, it's important to be seen to be leading the business change programmes that will ultimately result in culture change. Hands-on leadership ensures that your team knows what you're doing to contribute. You see, if you're a CEO or a senior leader in an organisation, most of your people don't know exactly what you do. They know you're the boss, but they don't know precisely what you do with your time. If you're trying to build an inclusive and open company culture, then it's important that your team understands your role and, ideally, sees you in action.

I like to share war stories with the team. Stories show very graphically that you understand what they go through day to day. They also illustrate that you are grappling with many of the same issues in your day-to-day activity as they are.

For example, if you call on a difficult customer, the salespeople will enjoy hearing the story of how the meeting went. Try to share with them some of the things that you were able to do to get a better outcome. Recounting the events becomes a learning experience for them too. If you got your butt kicked by the customer, tell them how it happened and how you felt. It'll make them feel better the next time it happens to them.

Most importantly, they will see that you're not just some person who sits upstairs in meetings. You become a colleague and someone who is out there dealing in a positive way with the same issues they are.

I like to make phone calls to customers in front of the salespeople. Whether it's a sales call or a response to a query or complaint, I like the fact that our salespeople will see me having to do the same difficult stuff that we are asking them to do. (Often, in their eyes, the leader is usually the most visible when doing the fun stuff.) Making those calls from the middle of the open plan area gets the message around the organisation quite quickly. It's not hard to do. Just walk up to someone's desk, ask if you can use their phone, and call the customer right there in front of everybody. Because people don't expect it, this

Believe it or not,
your people **don't understand
what you do**.

It's **your job** to help them
to **understand what you do** and
why you are relevant.

kind of approach can be an effective way of communicating the way you want people to respond.

I think it's really important to respond to customers who complain. I try to follow up any letter, email or phone call from a customer as quickly as I can. Usually I phone the customer, tell them I've received their letter or message, outline the things I need to do before I get back to them, and give them an idea of the timeframe involved.

Over the years, these direct customer experiences have provided me with countless stories to share with our teams. By sharing them, I'm letting the team know that I'm taking direct action to improve our performance in one of our critical target areas, in this case customer service. Of course I am, at the same time, keeping myself up to date with the needs and expectations of our customers or clients.

As your business grows, so it becomes harder for you to stay connected with your customers. It's a valuable lesson for all of us that we must interact regularly with our customers if we are to stay connected with the changing needs of their businesses and how those changes affect our business.

Culture change is really pretty simple. Like most things in business, it is first and foremost about being clear about what you're trying to achieve. Thereafter, it's about communicating with your people and ensuring that all parts of the business are acting in a manner consistent with those objectives. Developing a programme to continuously improve your performance in critical areas across the business and following through with it will result in cultural change over time.

✱ ✱ ✱

Standards support culture

We don't talk about standards in business often enough. To me, the establishment of standards enables us to set expectations with our people in terms of quality, responsiveness, behaviour and attitudes. Standards means doing things on time, on budget or being properly attired. It means company vehicles that are clean and driven responsibly. It means behaving in a manner that reflects the expectations of the company, its people and customers.

When I was in my CEO life, I almost always wore a suit, usually with a tie. Of course, in both the magazine business and the sports apparel company, our people wore every type of attire you could think of. Many, particularly the creative types — the designers, production people and writers, would often don T-shirts, jeans and sneakers for a day's work. Many of our suppliers and customers were

I'm intrigued that the taxi industry is complaining about Uber.
And yet most taxis are dirty, their drivers poorly presented, and they are often late, or, worse, fail to turn up when they have been booked in advance.
Surely, instead of complaining, that's where they have to start.

It's about standards.

intrigued as to the reasons for my often appearing to be overdressed. My response was always the same: 'If I wear a T-shirt, the troops will be in singlets!'

The standards set by the leaders within a business will reflect in the standards adopted by and the behaviour of the team. If the boss goes out for lunch every day and drinks a bottle of wine, don't be surprised if the troops expect to be able to do the same.

Standards extend to the drive for excellence. Excellent organisations feel let down if the behaviour of their people is less than it should be. High-performing teams are those with high standards. Again, we can look to sports for the analogies. Leading Formula One team McLaren Mercedes, New Zealand's rugby All Blacks, rugby league's Melbourne Storm, and European football heavyweight Barcelona are all organisations that demonstrate regularly high levels of performance. Behind the scenes they all require levels of diligence, preparation and presentation that place them ahead of their peers. If one of their people 'drop their guard', and standards slip, it can damage hard-won reputations and put the performance of the entire organisation at risk.

I recently received a letter from a third party who was seeking to do a major deal, in excess of $3 million, with one of our businesses. The two-page letter was from the company's CEO. The letter contained no less than 15 spelling mistakes, and was full of grammatical errors. You can call me pedantic if you wish. However, as stated elsewhere, first impressions count. Most, but not all, of his errors would have been picked up by a spell-check. His approach demonstrated a lack of attention to detail that would have been a major problem in the type of relationship he was suggesting. As a result, we politely declined his advances. A $3 million business opportunity lost because of spelling mistakes.

Here is a short list of questions to think about when contemplating the standards you maintain.

- How do your offices appear to the outside visitor? What does the garden outside the front door look like? Is the stairwell that leads to the bathrooms presentable?
- Your people can be your front window. How are your people presented? (Note, even if your people are changing tyres or repairing machinery, they can still be well presented in a manner that suits their business.)
- Your company vehicles are travelling billboards. Are your company vehicles clean and is damage to vehicles quickly repaired?

What do **outsiders** think when they **look at your business?** It doesn't matter how **shiny** the **policeman's uniform is** if the **police car is dirty.** **Public transport** that runs **late isn't a service.** It's a **nuisance.** Your **poorly attired employees** let down **the entire brand.**

- Do the people driving your vehicles understand the importance of driving responsibly in their 'travelling billboards'?
- How are visitors greeted when they enter your premises?
- What standards do you have in the office reception?
- When the company phone rings, how many rings is too many?
- Whose job is it to answer the phone when the receptionist is too busy to answer?
- Does the person answering the phone have pen and paper to take a message if they need to?
- Is the appearance of the website consistent with the appearance of the company's brand elsewhere?
- What do people's photos look like? (Real estate agents, motor vehicle dealers and investment bankers alike, take note.) If you are going to put photos of your people on the company's billboards, advertising or websites, or even their business cards, make sure they get good quality, and likeable, photos taken. (I know it sounds obvious, but if you doubt me, take a look at the photos on LinkedIn some time.)
- Do you have standards around the appearance of documentation and correspondence: spelling and grammar, letterheads and use of the company logo and brand logos?
- How are proposals presented? Do all salespeople use the same format?
- If you operate your business across geographical boundaries, how do you ensure that your cross-border clients receive the same service experience at every level, irrespective of which branch they are dealing with?
- As a retailer, are your stores appropriately presented?
- How are people remunerated? Is that fair and consistent?
- Do remuneration incentives align with the standards you are seeking to implement throughout the business?
- And finally . . . do you, the leader, live up to the standards you expect of your people every day?

Of course, the list of questions goes on. You can use this list to get started, but you're better to develop your own list as you go through your business, bit by bit. Ask the question. Do we know what we expect in this situation? What's important? If you don't have standards, you are leaving it up to others to decide what is important and what is appropriate.

Here's a suggestion: drive past a couple of high schools when the students are either leaving or arriving. Of course, most schools have uniforms. But it doesn't stop there. Ask yourself, 'How are those uniforms being worn?' Some schools have very

I recently travelled to the **USA**.
I couldn't help but notice the **presentation**
of some of the **male
United Airlines pilots**.
When you see an airline pilot with his **tie
at 'half mast'** and the **tail of his shirt
hanging out**, it makes you question that
person's standards and **judgment**.
When he's **flying my plane**, those are two
things that **I want him to be on top of**.

strict standards in terms of shirts being tucked in and socks being held up (boys) and dresses being a certain length (girls). As old fashioned as some of those rules might sound, stand outside such a school and compare the way they look to their neighbour down the road that doesn't share the same standards.

Now ask yourself, 'How would I prefer my team to look?'

Sometimes old-fashioned standards around presentation and behaviour are worth maintaining. Going back to those world-class sports teams, they will stand a player down for inappropriate behaviour or failing to observe a curfew. Players are disciplined if they are not dressed correctly. Would you do that in your business?

Maintaining standards can be tough. You need open support for the standards and consequences for failing to meet them. In fact, like values, standards can only be maintained in an environment where the people within the organisation are committed to them and the consequences for failing to abide by them are meaningful and effective. And yet again, you need to lead it from the top.

* * *

Values enable culture

We all have values. However, like people, some businesses have lousy values that have evolved from a negligent upbringing.

Alongside leadership and standards, values set the expectations in terms of behaviour within the organisation. A lot of organisations will set out a series of expected values, hang them on the wall in the lobby, and promptly forget about them. Others will spend days locked in a planning meeting deciding what the company values should be, only then to neglect the introduction of those values to the people that will be asked to live by them. Like culture, I believe that values evolve and come about as a result of the way you behave over time.

I am therefore not a fan of trying to prescribe upon your people what your values should be. Instead, I prefer to see an organisation that strives to operate at a certain level and aspires to do so in a certain way. In summary, your values are a description of how you behave as an organisation. Here are some headings to think about:

- How do we behave?
- How do we treat our people, our customers and our shareholders?
- What type of organisation do we want to be?
- Common words include honesty, integrity, equality, excellence, service, respectful, etc.

Everyone has **values**.
Even career **criminals** have **values**.
It's just that some people
have **lousy values**.
Some **businesses do too**.

What would you like your values to be?

A conversation

When I was in my early days at ACP, one of our managers approached me one day and asked to chat. She had been reading a business book, and came across a discussion about values in business. Her purpose in speaking to me was to ask the following question.

'What are our values?' she asked.

She went on to say that she had checked in our induction materials and couldn't find them written down anywhere.

I responded by saying that I didn't believe in writing down values that we weren't living up to, and I didn't think we were yet at a stage where the way we were behaving was worthy of being written down.

I asked her what she thought our current values were. Her comments concurred with my views. I then told her what I would like them to be one day. She agreed with my ambition, and added a couple of points that I had overlooked. She then agreed to let me know when she thought we were close to achieving the position that we both aspired to.

She came back to me 18 months later and said that she thought we could write them down.

* * *

One of the international companies I work with is The Drug Detection Agency (TDDA). TDDA specialises in workplace drug and alcohol testing, and they are a state-of-the-art market leader in both New Zealand and Australia. I am yet to see an executive in any organisation in any industry who is as committed to the company values as the CEO and founder is.

The following statements represent TDDA's vision, values and critical success factors.

The **quality** of a **leader**
is **reflected** in
the **standards they set**
for **themselves**.

Ray Kroc
McDonald's

> ## OUR VISION
> *Creating drug-free environments*
>
> ## OUR VALUES
> *Taking ownership with no excuses.*
> *Straight up, straight forward, no short cuts.*
> *Defining excellence through innovation, market leadership and integrity.*
> *Creating positive change in people's lives.*
> *People like us.*
>
> ## OUR CRITICAL SUCCESS FACTORS
> *1. Protect the girl on the bike (our ultimate customer)*
> *2. Branding (our calling card)*
> *3. Presentation of vans/offices (medical facility — perception is reality)*
> *4. Personal presentation (looking the part)*
> *5. Play by the rules (cross-border consistency of delivery)*
> *6. Treat people with respect (donors, clients, suppliers, colleagues, stakeholders, public)*
> *7. Our client is our absolute priority (going the extra mile)*
> *8. Do what's right (empathy, understanding, respectful)*
> *9. Leave nothing to chance (aim for perfection every time)*
> *10. The TDDA way (this is how we behave — our DNA)*

The reason I highlight this business is that the CEO of TDDA, Kirk Hardy, lives these values. Despite the fact that his people have heard the messages many times, he reiterates these messages at every opportunity. At every company conference, Kirk presents the Vision, Values and Critical Success Factors to his team of franchisees. He can be pretty passionate as he does so too. He also presents the same message to new franchisees, and members of the team who are attending training sessions.

Every year, Kirk and his management team conduct an annual review with every franchisee. Those meetings usually commence with him reiterating the values and critical success factors, what they mean and why they are important.

You might note, under the heading of Critical Success Factors, there is a reference

You can't just **hang** a '**values statement**' on the **wall** in reception and **expect** your **people** to **act in the manner described**.

First, you have to **earn the right** to have your people **act** in a **certain way**.

You do this through your own **messaging**, the way **you act** and the **conduct of the organisation**.

Then, and only then, can you **expect** such **behaviour** from your **people**.

to the 'girl on the bike' as their ultimate customer. This came about as a result of a news story that redefined TDDA's reason for being. A young woman was cycling to work early one morning when she was tragically hit by a truck and killed. It subsequently transpired that the truck driver had tested positive for drugs.

The people at TDDA are passionate about not allowing that to happen to cyclists or pedestrians who are overtaken by their clients. This is a company that lives its values by constantly referring to them at every opportunity. Many of the franchisees can recite these values by heart. But it doesn't stop the leaders from reinforcing the importance of them, as often as necessary.

Admittedly, the TDDA team is potentially dealing with life and death incidents. If they get it wrong, there could be a high penalty. However, their focus on getting it right gives them every chance of doing the best possible job for every customer, every individual who is drug tested and every person that those client companies come into contact with. So it's one thing to have your company values. It's another thing to live up to them.

* * *

Your values should summarise what is important to your organisation, the way you are expected to behave, and your commitments to your customers, your people and the community you work with. Values statements regularly use words such as 'excellence', 'integrity' and 'value'. A very typical generic values statement might read as follows:

> *Our values*
> *We believe the customer is our most important relationship.*
> *We recognise the value of every member of our team.*
> *We foster an environment of teamwork across our people and suppliers.*
> *We are respectful of and seek to contribute to our local community.*
> *Performing our role with excellence, integrity and trust is critical to our success.*
> *We are committed to achieving fair profits in return for delivering*
> *outstanding outcomes.*

Honesty, **integrity**, **treating people** with **respect**, **customer focus**. These characteristics, or values, should be **entry-level table stakes** for any **business**, and for anyone in a **leadership** or management role.

It takes time to grow into your aspirational values. As your business grows and develops, the role that you play as leader will influence the behaviour of your people. Sometimes you will sound like a 'broken record' repeating the same expectations over and over again.

You see, like the ACP example earlier, even if your values aren't written down, as a leader you can express your aspirations of what you want for your business. In doing so you can gently guide your people in terms of how you would like them to behave. As a result, you will move your team towards the values set that you are seeking.

And, as you know, the people in your team, and how they behave, will be critical to your success.

So think about it. What are your values today? What would you like them to be in the future?

Our Credo

We believe our first responsibility is to the doctors, nurses and patients, to mothers and fathers and all others who use our products and services. In meeting their needs everything we do must be of high quality. We must constantly strive to reduce our costs in order to maintain reasonable prices. Customers' orders must be serviced promptly and accurately. Our suppliers and distributors must have an opportunity to make a fair profit.

We are responsible to our employees, the men and women who work with us throughout the world. Everyone must be considered as an individual. We must respect their dignity and recognize their merit. They must have a sense of security in their jobs. Compensation must be fair and adequate, and working conditions clean, orderly and safe. We must be mindful of ways to help our employees fulfil their family obligations. Employees must feel free to make suggestions and complaints. There must be equal opportunity for employment, development and advancement for those qualified. We must provide competent management, and their actions must be just and ethical.

We are responsible to the communities in which we live and work and to the world community as well. We must be good citizens — support good works and charities and pay our fair share of taxes. We must encourage civic improvements and better health and education. We must maintain in good order the property we are privileged to use, protecting the environment and natural resources.

Our final responsibility is to our stockholders. Business must make a sound profit. We must experiment with new ideas. Research must be carried on, innovative programs developed and mistakes paid for. New equipment must be purchased, new facilities provided and new products launched. Reserves must be created to provide for adverse times. When we operate according to these principles, the stockholders should realize a fair return.

Postscript: Values

Johnson & Johnson's 'Our Credo' is widely regarded as one of the best examples of a values statement. I first came across it when we studied it at a university programme in the 1990s.

It was written in 1943, and yet today remains as relevant as ever. Unusually, it wasn't written by an academic, the marketing department, or the advertising agency. It was written by the Chairman, General Robert Wood Johnson. I have shared it on the opposite page. Consider the changes that have occurred in business over the last 75 or so years. Consider also the changes to the medical and healthcare industries that Johnson & Johnson has long been part of. The continued relevance of this document is something very special.

What's **important** is that you have **faith in people**, that they're basically **good** and **smart**, and if you **give them tools,** they'll do **wonderful things with them**.

Steve Jobs
Apple Computer

CHAPTER 7

It's About the People, Stupid

'If we treated our people as we would volunteers, the way we manage them would be very different; and in return those workers would deliver greater productivity and feel greater enjoyment. But instead, because we give them a paycheck, we assume we don't have to look after them. A paycheck can't buy passion.'

Paraphrasing Peter Drucker

I have paraphrased the statement above from the words of esteemed management consultant and author Peter Drucker. Many of his statements have become 'quotable quotes' including the following:

'Accept the fact that we have to treat almost anybody as a volunteer.'
'A paycheck doesn't buy passion.'

* * *

People make the difference

Business is all about people. As someone reportedly once said:

'The assets of a business go down in the elevator each evening.'

Product is **no longer** a point
of **difference**.

That means that you have to be
great at service.

And **service** means **people**.

It might be an old phrase, but it has never been more accurate. People should be every leader's number one priority. The observation above is truer now than ever before, because it's become increasingly difficult to differentiate products and even services.

Today, almost every business (with very few exceptions) is a service business. Yes, even those of you who are manufacturers. We live in an age where the great majority of products can be copied within 72 hours. Unless you are in a highly sophisticated and technical industry, and you have a completely unique and patented concept, supported by extraordinary levels of research and intellectual property, the chances are that your product can be copied by an Asian manufacturer or even someone at home with a 3D printer.

So having a great product is no longer a differentiator. And if you can't generate a point of difference through your product, the only alternative is to do so through service.

And service means people.

In other words, market differentiation is now determined by how quickly you can bring your products to market, the speed at which you can turn around a client request, or your ability to add value beyond the obvious things that your product shares with everyone else's.

So, while barriers to entry for most businesses are surprisingly low, and as a result, your product or service is no longer a point of difference, then your only chance at differentiation is through the way you interact with your customers, your team and other stakeholders.

People stuff.

As I've already mentioned, some of the newcomers brought to the international corporate scene reflect this. Uber doesn't own a taxi. Airbnb is the world's biggest hotel chain, and yet they don't own a hotel. They both bring a completely new service model to the market, with a totally different way of interacting with both their service providers and their customers.

Companies need to be responsive to be successful. Responsiveness means providing service. And in order to provide great service you need great people who are well qualified, informed and supported to enable them to do the job you are asking of them.

People hold the key to everything an enterprise does, whether it is interacting with customers, negotiating with suppliers or analysing budgets. The roles your people play are critical to the success of your business.

In most businesses, the importance of key people is sadly underestimated. As a result, the people within the enterprise are often not treated with the appreciation

Command and **control management structures** belong in the **1900s.** Your **people** are more **informed** and have their **own relationships** and **opinions.** You must **leverage** that to the **company's advantage.**

and respect they deserve. The performance of any organisation will only ever be as good as:

- the people you employ;
- the roles they occupy;
- the clarity under which they operate; and
- the tools available to them.

∗ ∗ ∗

Personnel engagement

The most recent generation of workers joining organisations over the past 15 years has dramatically altered the stature and importance of the people within the firm. Up until the mid-1990s, those with the seniority had the knowledge and experience. Workers down the line followed simple processes or did as they were told.

Life is not like that any more. Technology makes knowledge universal. Your people and your customers are more knowledgeable about almost everything. Leaders must, therefore, understand what messages are coming up through the organisation rather than focusing solely on the messages they may be sending down.

The industrial economy comprised products, hierarchies and buildings that were central to success. Now, knowledge, individual capability and personal relationships are the drivers of success in the new organisation. People, and not things, are paramount.

Previous generations of leaders and managers were able to operate with 'command and control'-based hierarchies due to the upbringing of yesterday's workers. Command and control is cheaper to operate. People are expected to do as they are told. 'Group-think' is the norm and getting one message to 100 people is straightforward. By contrast, close team management and one-on-one coaching and mentoring is time heavy and costly. But you do get better outcomes. Losing people is expensive too. The new worker will not respond to command and control.

Business has morphed over the last 60 years from 'command and control' management structures to team-oriented activity and open communication lines. But many of today's leaders and managers are still a product of the old-style approach.

If you think about the changes that many of us in business have seen, even in the last 20 years, and then consider the lack of adaptation by leaders and managers over that same period, we shouldn't be surprised by what we are hearing with increased regularity about the negative attitudes of our people to their work and their workplace.

Give your **people permission** to make a **difference**, and **they will**.

With **permission** comes **engagement** and **commitment**, which is followed quickly by **lower absenteeism**, improved **customer experiences**, and **greater productivity**.

As a result, terms like 'employee engagement' and 'personnel alignment' have become part of the current management speak. Such engagement is worst among those under the age of 35.

We know that with improved engagement of our people comes better productivity, lower absenteeism and less health and safety concerns. Improved customer experiences, lower personnel turnover and greater profitability follow.

If the business day is dull and predictable, it's hard to keep people interested, let alone engaged. They can become easily distracted.

In my consulting work, I see many businesses talking about personnel engagement and trying to measure workplace engagement. However at the same time:

- they are not telling their people what they are trying to achieve;
- they are not communicating goals, aspirations or progress;
- they are not sitting down one on one with their people and listening to what they think;
- they are not thinking about how younger members of the team might need to be managed and led;
- they are not giving meaningful induction to new team members;
- they are not offering training or retraining;
- what limited training is done is not followed up or supported, and so behaviours don't change;

. . . and we wonder why engagement is not improving!

As managers, we have to change. We need to be open, communicative, consultative, encouraging and involving if we want to engage all generations of our workforces and get the best out of our people.

The people that work within our organisations need to be given the permission to speak up and the ability to make the decisions that affect their teams and their customers. In return, they must be held accountable for the outcomes of those decisions and actions.

Success, they say, starts at the top. In my experience, that's true. But it also starts at the bottom, by getting the right people, in the right place, and doing the right things, right.

∗ ∗ ∗

The old **adage** that
"**people** are your most **important asset**"
is wrong.

People are **not** your **most**
important asset.
The **right people** are."

Getting the right people doing the right things, right

So, business owners or managers that want people to do a really good job for them — and who doesn't? — must first make sure that everyone on the team knows what the business is about and what management is trying to achieve.

This sounds pretty basic! It should be easy. There's just one problem: managers don't do it! Most managers try to manage without a plan. They go to work every day and react rather than initiate. Despite the enormous lump sums spent on management training every year, most managers verge on incompetent when it comes to leading people.

'Not me,' I hear you say. 'My people love me.'

That's what you think!

Consider this example.

Think about your last recruit. Did you spend enough time involved in the process to ensure you were making the right choice? Did you spend any time introducing the successful applicant to the business and talking about the company's priorities? Recruit selection is often an expensive mistake. All too often the new person is not up to the job or they need a great deal more training input than you had expected in order to bring them up to speed. Others end up compensating for the new recruit, at least for the time being. That results in the incumbent members of your team becoming annoyed with the new person from the outset.

I have lost count of the number of times I've been impressed by a company report or strategic plan, or listened to a CEO share their vision, plans and the opportunities they see for the future of the business, only to then encounter one of their people on a forecourt, in a store or (usually worse) on the telephone and realise that they have no idea what is going on in their business.

All too often we are guilty of appointing the wrong people to roles. It doesn't just happen with new people either. Most organisations are guilty at some time of the following sins:

- Recruiting a person from outside the company without doing appropriate levels of due diligence on the person — in many cases, not even pausing to check references;
- Recruiting a person from outside the company for a role that they are not equipped for;

Just because the **company aspirations** are outlined in the **annual report**, it doesn't mean that your **people understand them** or know how to **deliver to them**.

The **difference** between **statement** and **delivery** is the **communication gap**. Your job is to **close that gap**.

- Identifying a person from within the business and appointing them to a different role — often as a result of rushing to solve a problem or a vacancy, without fully considering the needs of the role or the capability of the person to perform it;
- Identifying a person who is underperforming in their current role within the organisation and moving them to an alternative position in order to solve a problem, without doing the necessary research on his or her capability for the new role, and then failing to provide the necessary training to support them.

These mistakes are made in business every day. When consulting at large companies I see it all the time. But it happens in small businesses too. And family businesses are among the worst. The close personal relationships in teams in small to medium-sized privately owned businesses frequently result in someone getting a job because they are a mate, or, alternatively, because we would rather move them than have a difficult conversation with them.

Recently, a large New Zealand business developed a plan to pitch to overseas organisations for substantial amounts of funding. The numbers being sought were well in excess of $100 million. The plan was critical to the success of the organisation and the funding was to be a cornerstone of the strategy going forward. As you would expect for a role of such importance, the decision was led by the CEO. They had a guy who was perfect — articulate, sophisticated, well presented, and well able to mix it with the large European investment funds. But he left. So they rushed to an alternative solution. The person they appointed to lead the project was knowledgeable about the requirements of the organisation, but was also notable for a number of other reasons:

- *He was not making progress in his existing role and something had to be changed;*
- *He had never done anything like it before — in fact, he had no experience interacting with the international investment community;*
- *His personal presentation was poor — he was overweight, and clearly had difficulty with clothing selection (think ill-fitting grey suit, black shirt, red tie);*
- *His presentation skills were appalling;*
- *He had no idea that he possessed any of these weaknesses.*

He was, however, good mates with the CEO and they trusted each other. Of

From the **first person** I **hired**, I was **never** the **smartest guy in the room**. And that's a **big deal**. And if you're going to be a leader, if you're a **leader** and you're the **smartest guy** in the world, **in the room**, you've got **real problems**.

Jack Welch
Former CEO
General Electric

course, it was a disaster. The initiative failed completely. There were expensive trips to the other side of the world, meetings set up with the right people, and so on. But despite a booming investment community and an appetite for Australia and New Zealand, no investment monies came forward.

I don't want to pick on the individual. It's important to remember that selecting him for this role was not fair to him. The fault lay squarely at the feet of the CEO, who in this case didn't understand what was really required for the role he was recruiting. He lacked the knowledge to make the right selection and should have sought assistance from recruitment consultants or other trusted allies to assist him in making such an important appointment.

The reason for this failure, and many like it that occur in business every day, was that they appointed the wrong person for the role. He was the wrong person to be fronting the international investment community. The cost of that decision to the organisation was immense. The entire strategy would fail without the funding.

We constantly see dumb companies making dumb decisions to send the wrong people to the wrong places, where they do the wrong things.

So how do we get better at people management?

* * *

Chances are that your **needs** have **changed** since you **last recruited someone** for a **particular role**.

So, before you go to the market for any role, **define** what that **position looks like today** and try to build a **picture** of the **type of person you now need**.

11 'R' words — how to be better at managing people

Over the years I have developed a framework for managing people issues, which the teams I have worked with have found to be useful. This little list of mine is intended to provide a checklist to ensure that we are doing all the things we should be as we go about the day-to-day responsibility of managing a team of people. Again, I believe it applies whether you have six people or six thousand.

Incidentally, these tips won't make you better at speaking in front of your team or cheerlcading them to greater outcomes. But they will help you improve the basics of people management.

1. Role definition

Everyone in the business should have a very clear description of what their position entails. And, if you are about to embark on a recruitment process, the best advice I can give is this. Be absolutely clear about the role you need to fill, the key skills required, and the ideal background you need the successful applicant to bring. This clarity is critical before you even decide whether you are likely to make an internal appointment or search externally. Before you start the recruitment process, you should try to answer the following questions:

- What type of person do we need?
- What key activities are involved?
- Are we replacing an existing role or is this a new role?
- If this is an existing role, how does this role vary from when we last recruited for it?
- If we get the right person, how can the role evolve and what does it look like in the future?
- What are the skills that the ideal person will bring to the role?
- If we look at the team this person will be part of, what skills is that team short on, and does this role give us an opportunity to overcome that weakness?
- What is their ideal personality?
- What is the ideal background for the successful applicant to have?
- Does this role ever involve difficult decisions or potential for conflict?
- What type of cultural mix within the team are we looking for?

When seeking a replacement, don't automatically look for a replica of his or her

Recruit slowly.

Choosing the wrong person
can be very expensive.

Terminate quickly.

Once you get it wrong, you have to put it
right promptly.

predecessor. The business has probably moved on since you last appointed someone to this role, so your needs may have changed.

Make sure that those team members who will interact with the new recruit understand what the new job definition looks like. Invite their input. As a result, the company's expectations are clear and the successful applicant now knows what's required and expected.

2. Recruit

Being clear about the type of person you are looking for enhances your chances of getting it right. My best advice is to take your time. Filling that role may be urgent, but here's the lesson I learned.

> *The best recruit I ever appointed was interviewed nine times.*
> *The worst? Five minutes.*

You might ask, 'How do you interview someone nine times?' Firstly, it was an important role. We were expanding our international sales business and we needed the right person to become our International Sales Director. We targeted a person out of the opposition, and once I knew he was interested, I had the typical initial meeting that lasted about 90 minutes. A week or so later, we met in a coffee shop and chatted for an hour or so. I then invited him to join me in a corporate golf day. We met formally again and talked some more about how we could make the role suit the skills of the individual. To keep the process moving, I met him for a drink one night after work, and not long after that, my wife and I invited him and his wife to dinner.

I'm not suggesting you need to do this for every appointment. This was a senior role and we were trying to get a senior guy off the opposition. But this rather protracted experience took only two months. You learn a lot about people by seeing them in different situations — watching how they treat waiting staff in a café or restaurant, or how they behave on a golf course, or whether their behaviour changes when their partner is present.

The best part of the whole process was that as I came to know him better, we were able to redefine the role to suit his skill set. In fact, we redesigned the role to suit what the market needed as a result of the candidate's own input. And with that amount of rigour in your process, as you would expect, this particular person was a great hire for our company.

Recruit slowly. Whatever the role, I recommend you meet the person at least

Make sure that **every new person understands** what the **company** is **trying to achieve**, who the **key people are**, and why their **role is important**.

three times before hiring. If it's a senior role, four or five times is probably more appropriate. Meet your favoured candidate in a number of settings. Sure, you should run the first session in a meeting room. After that, meet them for coffee or lunch. Observe how they interact with other people. Are they respectful or dismissive? Meet them for a drink at the end of the day and see how they act with a couple of drinks on board. If you are in a large company and recruiting a senior person or a member of your executive team, meet them with their partner over dinner. You will learn a lot and also get an opportunity to 'sell' the partner on the employment opportunity.

Remember, the cost of getting it wrong is invariably high, so spend the time on the process to get it right.

3. Rules (induction)

Induction doesn't stop at the coffee pot and a bathroom tour. New people need time and space to understand the business and how they fit.

Make sure people are fully inducted into the ways of the enterprise. They need to know who's who, key clients, expected behaviours, the goals and objectives of the business and how their role contributes to its overall success. Too few companies do this really well. And, like many other things, it's not difficult to do. We just have to do it.

A person's loneliest day is often their first. Make sure a new person is not left sitting alone at lunch time on their first day. You want them to feel part of the team. Go sit with them or, better still, take them to the local café for lunch. Introduce them to others. And most of all, encourage your team to talk to the new people. (This is most important with the millennial generation — see next chapter.)

Remember what your first day was like. It can be lonely. Good leaders make people feel welcome and informed so they immediately feel comfortable in their new environment. That comfort ties them in to your organisation for a longer term and they'll be better members of the team as a result.

4. Remuneration

First, make sure you are paying a fair base salary or wages for the job. This will influence attitudes. People must feel like they are an important part of the business. To establish that, they must feel valued, and that includes feeling that they are fairly remunerated.

Then, on top of a fair level of base pay, try to structure some component of performance-based remuneration. Every role in a business can contain an element

How many times do you **interview people** for the **six most critical roles** in your **business**?
(**Note**: Anything **fewer** than **four** is **not enough**.)

of incentive-based remuneration. Even administration and support people can share in performance success. Something as simple as a few $100 notes at Christmas time will result in a smile you will never forget and loyalty you can never repay.

In their 2005 work 'The Office of Strategy Management', Harvard Business School's Robert Kaplan and David Norton reported that 67% of HR managers agreed that HR and remuneration (incentives) strategies were not aligned with business unit and corporate strategies. They went on to say that the compensation packages of the majority of middle managers had no link to the success or failure of strategy implementation.

In most of our businesses we can keep this simple. But we should try to pay a fair base remuneration that's coupled to an incentive structure, and we should see to ensure that the incentive is aligned to that person's contribution to the achievement of the company's key objectives. Make sure that each individual understands how he or she contributes to the organisation's success, and reflect that in their incentive programme.

5. Recognise

We all thrive on recognition. It's always easy to recognise salespeople for their performance. Most companies do so with bonuses, incentives and even overseas trips. However, the rest of the team members are also contributing and it's important to come up with creative ways of also shining the spotlight on those who aren't involved in the sales effort.

Try recognising people for even the smallest of things. A handwritten congratulatory note for a job well done or a birthday card on the appropriate day can work wonders. Even the boss stopping by a workstation and asking about the family helps. Or maybe ask about the triathlon they did on the weekend or the little league team they coach.

It may be as simple as a Friday morning tea to celebrate a birthday or the completion of some extramural study. Take an interest in and recognise your people for what they do inside and outside the business.

6. Reward

Catch people doing good things, then find ways to make a presentation of a suitable reward. Acknowledge success with small celebrations regularly. A $20 bottle of wine or a restaurant voucher for two for a job well done can go a long way.

My mother's generation had some great sayings that had been handed down by their parents. One was 'It's the thought that counts.' As leaders, we often fail to appreciate how much these things can mean to people.

Everyone in the business must have some form of **performance-based incentive**. It doesn't have to be **a lot**. Just something to **celebrate** their **contribution** to your **goals**.

I was once approached by a very quiet and unassuming member of our team. His work on a particular project had led to our recognising him with a $150 dinner voucher for two people. He was delighted by the gesture, but because dining out didn't happen often in his family, and was thus seen as something of a special occasion, he asked if he could use his voucher at a low-cost chain restaurant so he could take his three kids. That's how much it meant to him.

People need to know they are appreciated. One of the firms I'm involved with, by the nature of the industry, is heavily focused on health and safety. They work hard to avoid any long-term employee injuries (LTIs). For every quarter that the company is LTI free, around 300 people receive a $40 voucher. Do you think they focus on safety? You bet they do, and the teams get very excited when they achieve their health and safety goals. It happens because the company makes the safety goal important and rewards good behaviour.

7. Reveal (communication)

My thoughts on the importance of communication have already been well documented. Communicating with your people is crucial. It matters little how small or large your team may be. But getting key messages through to everyone is seemingly hard to do.

You must let everyone know what's going on, what's working well and where you have some challenges. Your people need to understand what's important. And they need to know how they contribute to the goals of the organisation.

The best person to solve a problem is the one working closest to it. Your people need to know that a problem is important to you, and that they have your permission to help fix it. Similarly, they need to be able to go after opportunities on your company's behalf. However, for people to do their best on your behalf when interacting with your clients, they must be informed.

Communication doesn't just mean emails and newsletters. It means getting out and about, talking to your people in both formal and informal settings. Big room meetings and casual stops in the open plan are all part of the communication mix. How you communicate is up to you, but you can never overdo it.

8. Retrain

Educationalists say they are trying to prepare today's students for tomorrow's jobs that don't yet exist. It's a nice way to sum up the speed of change. Most jobs will change dramatically over the next three years. It's crucial, therefore, to keep people

Catch people doing something right!
Celebrate them.
Reward them.
Praise them.

at the forefront of developments in the industry and business in which they work.

As managers, we must either constantly change our people to deal with the new skills required — which sounds expensive and is not a strategy I'd recommend — or constantly train and upskill our existing workforce to improve their capability and prepare them for the changing environment. Helping people to develop new skills keeps them motivated and more engaged. Any form of training forces people to think outside the box. It also helps them to be more creative when looking at the issues and opportunities they see around them every day.

As business continues to change at a rapid pace, it makes sense that the roles our people undertake will change as well. We need to be conscious of keeping them prepared for what they come up against each day.

9. Review

Of all the personnel and employee surveys I have read, one thing stands out. Inevitably, 75% or more say that they have never had a review, or even received meaningful feedback. At least half meet with their manager as part of their team less often than once per month.

Your people must have the opportunity to sit down for a formal one-on-one review with their direct manager at least twice a year. Two-way reviews that canvass feedback on the individual's performance and their views on the performance of the business are invaluable.

The purpose of the performance review is to create an opportunity for a manager and a member of his or her team to get together and discuss performance. Note, I didn't say whose performance. Performance reviews should be two-way. We (managers) should be discussing the performance, expectations and aspirations of each of our people in a meaningful way. However, we should also be listening to their views on the performance of the business and us as their managers in particular.

Leaders should sit down with their key people every six months. Talk openly about their job performance and relate it to the company's goals. Invite them to share their views about the business. Your people will tell you whether you're meeting your clients' and other stakeholders' expectations much more accurately than a profit and loss statement or balance sheet.

Stay away from the old-style 16-page performance review favoured by even older-style human resource (HR) managers. Just sit down and talk to your people. You must try to find out what they think about their role and the business as a whole. You can, in the process, share your thoughts on areas that you believe they need to work on. But don't make them complete a 16-page questionnaire in advance and

Give your people **good**, **constructive**, **timely feedback**. If you **don't**, they **won't learn** ... and they **won't improve**.

then discuss their answers. That's not a review; it's a survey.

Use simple questions to make your people comfortable and get the discussion going. Here are some suggestions:

- How do you think it's going?
- What do you think we are doing really well as a company?
- What do you think we need to work on?
- In what areas do you think that you are doing a really good job?
- Are there things that you feel you are struggling with?

Non-confrontational. Simple. Conversation starters that make your people feel comfortable about contributing to the discussion. Sure, if you have issues with some of the things an individual is doing, you need to raise them and discuss them in a constructive manner. But both of you will get more benefit out of a conversation than you will out of a one-sided lecture.

Have a look at the postscript at the end of this chapter for more ideas about questions you can ask to make your performance reviews more effective.

10. Respect

People spend a lot of time at work. Usually they want to do a good job. As the leader or manager, the better you can inform and support them, the more they contribute to what you are trying to achieve.

Always try to give your team time to deal with changes. Remember, they are not as informed about what is going on in the business as you are, so the risk of uncertainty on their part is higher. Do everything you can to keep people informed. We need to acknowledge that people are busy in their lives, and may not always get to the office by 9 a.m., and sometimes they might have to leave before 5 p.m. From time to time, they will need to visit a doctor, physio or pharmacy during work hours. And if they do, it won't kill your business. If your people are doing a good job for you, it doesn't hurt to be a bit flexible around some of these issues.

In particular, always treat those people who are leaving — it doesn't matter whether they are doing so of their own volition, or whether their departure is a result of a company decision — with the respect that you would hope to be treated with if you were in their position. If you go through tough times, then treat those asked to leave with as much respect and compassion as you can.

Last year I was advised of a guy that had left his senior sales role at one of

Always treat your people

with **respect**.

And remember, their **workmates**

are **watching**.

the media sales companies. He had been with the company for almost ten years and was one of their top performers. He had decided to leave of his own accord. Upon advising the company of his resignation, something highly unusual happened for a person of such stature within the sales team. Nothing.

His final day came. There was no morning tea, no presentation and not even a farewell of any sort. In fact, a couple of his workmates organised a few drinks down the road after work on his last day and that was it.

When it came to receiving his final pay a few days later, it was incorrectly calculated. At first he was told that his calculations were wrong. Then the story came down that the company wouldn't pay him. As I understand it, the difference was a couple of weeks' holiday pay. He had to argue with the company for two months before they agreed to pay.

What does this sort of behaviour by management say about their respect for their people? It says everything. They have none. We need to treat people as well on the way out as we do on the way in. Firstly, it's just a better and nicer way to do business. But remember too that those people remaining are the former workmates of those who have left. You have to remember that your remaining team members are watching how you deal with people who are their friends.

I have to admit that I get really disappointed when good people resign. I shouldn't, but I take it quite personally. I take it as a rejection of the things that we are trying to do. Nevertheless, we have to put a brave face on (after trying to talk them out of it), thank them for the contribution they have made and wish them well.

My message is simple. Irrespective of the circumstances of their departure (serious misconduct notwithstanding), treat people with respect as they leave.

Respect for the individual doesn't stop at the people who are or have been inside your company. Spare a thought for the people you deal with who are external to your business. One group that comes to mind is unsuccessful job applicants. We know that people will apply for a job with an organisation, and sometimes even get an interview, only to be unsuccessful. However, all too often those people never receive a response. They end up 'assuming' that they didn't get the job. Part of respecting them is to get back to them, thank them for applying, let them know why they were unsuccessful, and provide them with constructive feedback that may help them next time. Even if they fail, the experience that this group of people have when they engage with your company will impact the way they feel and talk about you.

Respect also means acknowledging that people have a life outside work and that you're grateful that the good ones still want to work with you. Let them know how

Managing people for greater engagement

Role definition

Recruit (slowly)

Rules (induction)

Remuneration

Recognise

Reward

Reveal (communication)

Retrain

Review

Respect

Retain

you feel. And, finally, think about the terminology you use when talking about your people. Some will take offence at words like 'staff' and 'subordinate'. As you may have noticed, I prefer to call them 'people'.

11. Retain

You can't afford to lose any of your greatest assets after putting so much work into them. Losing good people is expensive. Replacing them is often difficult and time consuming. It is always preferable to keep the ones you already know and trust.

Consider how you would feel about working in the business and think about the things that would keep you there. Always try to understand what your people are going through at an operational level and look for ways to make their day better. Try to identify a few trustworthy members of the team to act as touchstones — people who you can talk to regularly to get the mood of the wider team.

As a result of building better relationships with your people 'at the coalface', you might identify the need to provide better equipment or additional tools or facilities, which involves cost. However, you will be doing so on a much more informed basis. Alternatively, there may not be any additional resources needed, but the value you create by taking the time to get to know your people, show that you care about them, and demonstrate that you value what they do for you, is impossible to calculate.

Based on my experiences, being a more people-friendly leader is not overly difficult. You won't get on with everyone. But, with the distractions around us every day, you must constantly remind yourself of your people's needs. Being aware of the 11 points above will make you a uniquely good employer.

MBWA

Management
by
Wandering
Around

Wander, observe, ask and listen — MBWA

In Search of Excellence, co-authored by McKinsey & Company management consultants Tom Peters and Bob Waterman, was one of the most successful business books of the 1980s. It's still considered one of the best of its genre ever written. It contained, among its eight profound leadership lessons, one in particular that the giant American high-tech company Hewlett-Packard gave us. It was called 'management by wandering around', or MBWA for short.

As a former Hewlett-Packard dealer I was, in those days, a big fan of the company. Sadly, as a result of their hideous merger with another computer company, Compaq, my admiration has faded. However, I digress. Back in the 1980s, after reading about MBWA in Peters and Waterman's book, I took the concept seriously. To me it meant being visible, accessible and available to your people and your clients and keeping your eyes open to what's going on in the business.

To communicate successfully with their people, leaders must:

- be available
- be accessible
- be visible
- speak once, listen twice
- listen, listen, listen
- follow up on what you learn from every interaction.

I really enjoy working with mid-sized companies. You know the type: those with turnover between $20m and $100m and between 50 and 300 people. There I often find focused, capable leaders who are reasonably successful and working hard to build up their privately held or family business. They have usually worked hard over a long period to attract and retain a few good people.

Within these businesses I often find a willingness to soak up and act on any lessons that someone like me can give and a responsiveness which means that things 'happen' much more quickly than in a corporate environment.

One of those companies is MOVE Logistics, a transport, logistics and warehousing company operating throughout the country from its base in Christchurch, New Zealand.

The founder is Brendan Prendergast, or BP, and he is one of the best MBWA operators I know. Always on the move (no pun intended), BP is a 'perpetual motion' kind of guy. He is constantly visiting MOVE's various warehouses, continually

The 7 Habits of the Engaged Leader:

Accessible

Visible

Interactive

Observant

Inquisitive

Interested

Responsive

meeting with his key clients, and regularly dropping in on his team.

He's even on the road at 5 a.m. some mornings, driving out to the countryside to visit his drivers who have respectively travelled from opposite ends of the country to swap over trucks on the daily milk run.

Most managers can't tell you who their top 10 clients are. But BP can. He can name them, refer to the last meeting he had with them, identify whether there are any current issues, and probably tell you when he's next due to catch up with them for a beer after work. As a result, he is highly informed about any issues and opportunities facing his business.

The knowledge gained from his wanderings comprises a large part of MOVE's unique competitive advantage. Every leader running any business would do well to emulate BP's MBWA disciplines.

Being accessible and visible and listening carefully should be every leader's top-of-mind reaction at every level in today's business environment. As leaders, we should constantly ask ourselves:

'What am I going to do today to interact with my people?'

Over the years, I've been really conscious of the need to embrace the MBWA approach. Here are some of the ideas that I've tried to improve my performance in this area.

At Colliers, I was constantly on the road visiting our 15 offices in Australia and New Zealand. I listened to people, got out and repeated the message about the state of the business, and tried to remind everyone what we were trying to achieve. I listened, looked for solutions to problems that existed in our various offices and then, through understanding, was able to explain how we had solved similar problems elsewhere in other parts of the business.

Through this process I also came to know our people well, despite the fact that they were spread throughout Australia and New Zealand — an area that is geographically larger than the USA. Over time, I was also able to galvanise the support of the senior people from many of our offices, and as a result we built a team of people who could carry the core messages rather than just me.

My constant travelling ensured that we were able to monitor performance across a number of business units and look for opportunities to cross-sell ideas, clients and geographic differences.

So, **get out on the road** and **talk to your people**, your **customers**, and your **customers' customers**, and find out what people **think of your business**, how they **interact** with your **company**, and how they **use** your **products**.

It's hard to be visible across 15 offices in two countries, but, equally, it was something I was very conscious of.

At ACP we had different challenges. We tried to strengthen a weak corporate culture through quarterly full company meetings designed to communicate performance. It is, however, difficult to generate questions and feedback from people when they're sitting in a large audience of workmates. Even more so when one third of them are journalists, many of whom were not the most forthcoming group.

So we also set up weekly morning teas, where I met with our people in small groups and they would set the agenda while I brought the muffins or cookies. The objective? To talk openly about the things that our people wanted and needed to discuss.

Our weekly morning teas were really successful in breaking down an untrusting culture and helping me to see the challenges that our people were having, first hand. They also gave me the opportunity to share my side of the story and to build support for our plan.

Picking up an idea from the real estate business, we also instigated quarterly business reviews that brought everyone together to discuss the performance of each individual magazine, website or product line. We talked about editorial performance, cost management, magazine sales, advertising and production and other issues. It took a week every three months to go through the quarterly business review of our 55 publications and their associated online platforms. It was worth every moment.

On a lighter, but no less important, note, it was at ACP that I started to either visit or call every person in the company on their birthday. Did you know, there are businesses comprising just five people in which the leader has no idea of when any of them are having a birthday? Simple it may be, but remembering and acknowledging someone's special day makes a big impact on people.

In fact, the birthday calls became something of an event in themselves, and I must admit, I underestimated just how important it had become to some of the people. With 500 or so people, I guess there was always a chance of getting it wrong. And sometimes I was guilty of calling on a birthday celebrant a day early, or, worse, a day late. In most instances people understood. However, when I missed one completely, I was made to understand the impact that this rather simple act had on people. On this occasion, I bumped into one of our deputy editors, a wonderfully talented journalist and a terrific person, in the open plan area and I was pointedly given the 'silent treatment'. It turned out that my system had failed me and I had completely missed her birthday. I suspect that there was a bit of mischief in her reaction, but she had the right to feel a bit miffed. I felt terrible and I have never forgotten it.

Quarterly reviews create an opportunity for you to sit down with the **people** who can **influence the performance** of a **product**, a **division** or a **territory**. These sessions enable you to **review** what's **going well** and **what's not**, with the **people responsible** at a time when the events are all current in everyone's mind. Keep the numbers to **eight people or fewer**, and **encourage** everyone to **participate openly**.

There's no doubt in my mind that simple actions by people in leadership roles like celebrating birthdays or noticing something special is happening with your people can break down and repair an uncooperative culture.

> *When it comes to celebrating birthdays, I'm not as good as Stephen Collins. Stephen was one of the founders of the Australasian real estate group Harcourts. During his long tenure as CEO, one of the many unique 'people-centric' things he did was call every Harcourts person on their birthday. He then sang 'Happy Birthday' to them over the phone! Can you believe your CEO doing that? In those days his company had just over 2000 people. That's just over five calls a day, on average. It's interesting that Harcourts had a personnel turnover of just one-third of the industry average during his tenure.*

I followed my Colliers lessons when I joined Canterbury International. I travelled constantly to ensure that our people, our international clients, partners and other stakeholders were informed about the company's performance and activities, and to show them that they had access to the leadership. The travel also meant that I was always informed of the issues across a global business.

Two thirds of the entire 600-plus Yellow Pages team were salespeople. We instituted a regular Monday morning sales meeting at which I, as CEO, was always present and trying to contribute.

Again, my goal was to visit every office every quarter. I only made it about three times a year because the company's funding issues were, to put it bluntly, frequently all-consuming. When I was at our Auckland head office, where more than half of our team were based, I would block out time in my diary, at least twice a week, to spend a couple of hours walking the floor and chatting to the troops, particularly those in the sales organisation.

Based on these experiences, out on the floor talking to your people, and creating an environment in which they feel comfortable approaching you and talking to you; sharing ideas and discussing the issues that confront them as they dealt with clients every day, makes a huge difference. The more exposed they are to you, the more likely it is that your people will grow to accept you, be comfortable around you, and be willing to give you feedback and support. But here's the most important bit. By sharing their experiences, the people I have worked with have greatly enhanced my knowledge about what was going on in the business, all because I made it a priority to get out and about.

After leaving Yellow, and with the banking syndicate having assumed ownership,

What is the most **important day** in the
lives of your **people**?
It's probably their **birthday**.
What will you do for them that
'blows them away'?

I noticed a large number of people were also leaving the business. People kept asking me to provide verbal references for them as they sought to get traction with potential new employers. I was always happy to do so. After one such reference proved successful, one of our former team members was appointed to a new role in a major technology company and he took me out for a drink to say thank you. During our conversation I mentioned the number of people leaving and asked him why the exodus?

'Do you remember when you were there, you were always at the sales meetings and often walking through the open plan, talking to us?' he said. 'We always felt like we knew what was going on, that you were interested, and you were even able to help us with client calls sometimes. We haven't seen anyone from upstairs since you left.'

This was, I think, as good a compliment as any leader can receive. Your people notice this stuff.

MBWA has one major advantage. You get to know your people well and you know what's important to them. You also know who's performing and who isn't. If you're a good judge of people, you can tell by meeting them and getting to know them, which ones are capable and which ones are all talk.

Recently I bumped into one of our former salespeople at the pool where I swim. She was one of our top people in a company I had worked closely with and she regularly made the annual sales achievers trip. She was very bright, highly capable and had succeeded in a number of different roles. I had come to know her well through my wanderings, and subsequently through our mutual participation in the various get-togethers for our top achievers.

When I met her, I asked how things were going at the firm. She advised me that she was no longer there. She went on to tell me that she had been made redundant as a result of the company discontinuing a product line. Here was a person who was one of our top salespeople, irrespective of what product line she was representing, being let go.

I remember being surprised at the time, thinking to myself, 'You never let your top salespeople go.'

A few weeks later I bumped into two of my former colleagues, one of whom had led the redundancy programme. I asked about the staff cuts, and received a full and frank update of what had happened and why.

You have to make every effort to get to know **ALL** of your **people**. The more you **understand them**, and the better you **know them**, the **less likely** you are to make **stupid people decisions**.

Purely out of interest, I asked about my friend from the pool and the reasons for her departure. To my surprise, they didn't know and were surprised to find out that one of their top sales performers had been released. My former colleague could not even recognise her by name. The new leadership team didn't know her.

This was not even a huge company. Six hundred people in total. And as it turned out, she was just another name on the list.

If you don't know what's going on in your business, and you don't know who's important, you end up making dumb decisions.

Regular MBWA protects you from making dumb decisions.

Finally, a few thoughts on just how important follow-up is to people. If discussions with your people require you to take action, it is really important to follow up promptly. Take the necessary action and then communicate back to everyone concerned and tell them what's been done.

Some of the women in our ACP team worked late at night, particularly around deadlines. Understandably, they wanted a brighter light in the car park. As noted earlier, the problem came to my attention during one of our morning teas, and cost just $1,178.00 to solve. At Yellow, our salespeople often needed help with a difficult customer. That sometimes resulted in my calling the client to try to create a better opportunity for the salesperson. Persistent production problems at Canterbury often called for my involvement in the hope of finding a better outcome. At Colliers, I frequently led new business pitches alongside my teammates from the local office.

I learned about all these things and was able to identify ways to help by wandering around and interacting in various ways with people inside the organisations I've led. My conclusion is simply this: If you don't get out and talk to your people, you won't learn from them and you won't be able to contribute to their success.

* * *

Most **managers** are **reluctant** to have **close-up conversations** with their **teams** because they are **afraid** of what **people might ask for**.

In 20 years of morning teas, the **most expensive thing** I was ever **asked for** was an additional **light in the car park**. It cost just **$1,178.00**.

Caring for your people

Leaders and managers must, if they want their enterprise to truly succeed, do more than pay lip service to the adage that people are their business's single greatest asset. Your people should be treated like diamonds and cared for accordingly.

Caring for your people makes good sense in a multiplicity of ways. Conversely, investing time, effort and money finding, developing and retaining good people and then failing to properly care for them, makes no sense at all. But we all have to remember the following: even the best people sometimes hit on hard times and need some extra care and attention.

Managers who help their people when, for one reason or another, the going gets tough, perform a service more valuable than any earnings before interest, tax, depreciation, and amortization (EBITDA) model can ever measure.

Our people struggle with all sorts of challenges in their lives. I've listed some of the personal challenges, both major and minor, that I've encountered when dealing with our people over the years. They can include:

- their house sale falls through;
- they believe their job is at risk;
- there's been a family suicide;
- they're exposed to drug or addiction problems;
- they're exposed to alcohol abuse;
- abusive relationship problems exist;
- they are having difficulty with elderly parents;
- a son or daughter has died or had a serious accident;
- financial problems and bankruptcy;
- they're dealing with the consequences of an earthquake or other natural disaster;
- they've been injured or had an accident.

As a leader or manager who cares about people, you can't leave them high and dry to deal with this stuff. It may be expensive and take time to deal with, but, as a caring and enlightened leader, you should act. And do you get payback from your people when they see you doing the right thing by their peers? Absolutely.

Some people in your organisation may be a lost cause. But when things get tough, others in the team will come through. As a leader, you should always try to care about your people and offer to help them when it's needed. But, your people must also help themselves. It is not just the impact on the individual that's facing

When was the **last time** you took a **new person** out to **lunch on their first day**?

problems that creates value for you as a manager, leader or employer. There is genuine organisational value in having those members of your team who are watching on know that, if they were in the same position, you would look after them too.

I believe in the value of holding on to your people and treating them well, and I would like to see managers making greater efforts to do just that. After all, it's better for the business, and keeping people in their jobs is another way of caring for them. I see many businesses with good people trying to do their best, but managers failing to appreciate just how well they're doing. Leaders who can't be bothered are often the root cause of the problem.

People in the recruitment industry often tell me about companies where the staff turnover runs at 50%. In other words, half the people leave the business every year. Conventional wisdom states that it costs 40% of a person's annual salary to lose them and replace them. That means that uncaring management gets expensive. Even if you are running a small business with 12 people earning an average of $60,000 a year, a 33% personnel turnover will cost the business $96,000 per year. I don't think there are too many 12-person businesses that can afford that.

The problems I see aren't restricted to small businesses. One that I know of employs 650 people and is running a 50% staff turnover ratio. They must be doing something wrong. It's not even a difficult business to manage, operating mainly in the technology space. But the CEO is not, sources say, a nice person to deal with, and he has a reputation for not giving a damn about his people.

Caring leaders create opportunities. I'd like to see a campaign calling out for 'brave leaders'. I'm talking about people with good communication skills and great ideas who are willing to make a difference through better management. They're the people who will take reasonable risks to make their business a better place in which to work and enable their people to perform better. I'd also like to see a business owned and operated totally by people over 55 years of age. Not because I don't value young people. I do. But I know that a lot of people over 55 have good experience and knowledge, and a great work ethic, and yet find it hard to get work. How cool would it be to change that by creating opportunities for those people?

I've written already about trying to be better at the things we can control. This is one of those things. Creating an environment in which your people respect you for your leadership approach, understand what the company is trying to achieve, and feel free to ask questions about areas of the business that concern them, is not difficult to do. That environment can, however, have an enormous impact on the job satisfaction of your people, on their belief in the company, and, of course, dramatically reduce your personnel turnover rates.

I remember flying to Christchurch the day after the first Canterbury earthquake in 2010.

I was deliberately one of the first people into the office on the Monday morning.

I was picking the TV up off the lunchroom floor when people started arriving in numbers.

Of our 70 Christchurch-based team members, six had been badly affected. I remember that one had completely lost her house, her dad was overseas, and she didn't know what to do.

Others just needed a talk and maybe even a hug.

I had one-on-one conversations with everyone who wanted or needed one.

With no expectation of repayment, we gave out some financial relief to those who really needed it. I think we responded really well. But it felt totally inadequate.

Sometimes you will do all you can, but it is never enough.

Let me assure you of this one thing. When your corporate career is over, you will ultimately forget the financial outcomes, the strategy documents and quite possibly the bonus cheques. You will maintain some of your relationships but many, with common interests no longer common, will wither. What you will remember, however, is the people you helped. In fact, when you boil it all down, good leaders change the lives of the people they work with. That's a big responsibility.

$$* * *$$

Motivation — what drives your team?

It is, at this point, important to understand what it is, exactly, that motivates and drives people. As a leader, you need to have a good feel for what you believe drives you personally and also understand, at least in general terms, what motivates the people you lead. Communication is, as I've said earlier, fundamental to effective leadership. But it's equally important for you, as a leader, to understand why and how people are motivated by your communications.

The last 30 years have delivered astonishing insights into how the brain functions and, consequently, a better understanding of how people learn. According to the experts, people learn in many different ways.

Some absorb pages of text simply by reading. Others learn best through repetition, or rote, which you may recall teachers once used to implant times tables in our brains. Pictures, rather than words, work best for some, as they create mind maps and use colourful drawings to help them to learn or grasp a topic. Others use a combination of all methods. Understanding how we each learn best is important. Even teenagers now recognise their learning strengths and weaknesses and how they best absorb information.

There is, however, much less discussion about the different ways by which people are motivated. Perhaps that's because it's less complicated but it's certainly no less important. Understanding how and why people are motivated is much more important to a manager than understanding how they learn.

I'm no psychologist, but I've worked with thousands of colleagues over the years and been pleasantly surprised and alternatively highly frustrated by many of them. The upside of my experiences is that I have, I believe, developed a feel for 'what makes people tick' and what drives the activity and performance of some individuals and teams alike. Listed below are a few of the more common personal motivational drivers that I have observed over the years.

You might, as you read, be reminded of people you've worked with (as I have

Most of your people will
be **doing their best**.
If there's a **failure**,
blame the **performance**,
not the **performer**.

been while I've written this). It could be interesting to compare the characteristics of their behaviour with my comments. Note, this is not intended to be a complete list of personality types. These are merely my own unscientific thoughts and categories based on my experience. Specialists in this area will, no doubt, offer more categories and greater depth of knowledge and insight around each.

But I think it's something that leaders should be trying to understand, and this modest list should provide a starting point to satisfy a typical manager's most common needs.

SELF-DRIVEN

Some people are absolutely driven. They are focused, set goals, work extremely hard and are energised by everything they do — be it learning, sporting or work-related. These people are often frustrated by slow progress or by others around them who don't keep up. And look out if job promotions don't come their way soon enough. They're usually impatient high achievers who put great pressure on themselves to succeed.

Many self-driven individuals are often well suited to individual rather than team sports. In team sports, the self-driven individual often gets frustrated by the failures of others around them and can feel that other team members are not trying hard enough. Self-driven individuals can, on the other hand, be ideal candidates to lead a team, particularly where high performance is a desired outcome. There's a risk, however, that self-driven individuals can get offside with poor performers. But, if they gain and maintain their team's respect and support, they frequently get difficult projects completed successfully and on time.

TEAM DRIVEN

Team players are usually driven by a desire to not let others down. These individuals work best in a team environment. Think about study groups, sports teams and working group cells. These people do everything they can to make the team or group successful. They'll sometimes even cover up or, in some way, compensate for the group's underachievers. In sport, these people operate at a different level to the rest of the team, but not for the individual plaudits. Their motivation comes from striving to never let others down and ensuring that the team succeeds.

The team-driven individual copes with loss so long as it's not them personally who has let the team down. In a business environment, these individuals are well suited to managing tasks and projects in areas of accountability where everybody in the team must deliver. They often act in a 'sweeper' role to ensure that the detail is captured or completed. A team player is, however, often comfortable

At the **end** of your **career**, you might **forget the jobs**, the **titles**, the **PowerPoint presentations**, and possibly even the **bonus cheques**.

You will **never forget** the **people** you helped.

operating as a team member who is also very focused on ensuring that the right outcome is achieved.

Leaders can, obviously, be driven by wanting the team to do well or even by a need to protect them. I recall some of the dark days at Yellow when we feared that the whole business could collapse. The really powerful motivator that kicked in was an overwhelming desire to save everyone's jobs. It became about the people, not the bankers.

Team-driven people make great leaders. Of course, they have to be good at all the technical aspects of their role, but they don't have to be the star. They are the 'glue'; the person who holds it all together when things get difficult. We see plenty of these people in sport. In New Zealand it was recently retired rugby player Richie McCaw. Australia's rugby league captain, Cameron Smith, bears the same qualities. Neither is flashy. But both are there for the good of the team they lead.

I admire people who can cross over from a team to an individual sport and do well at both. People are, it seems to me, motivated in different ways as they approach different events or even different stages of their life. There is no question that our motivational drivers alter as we become more experienced and encounter different challenges.

FEAR DRIVEN

A fear of failure motivates many of us. This group can sometimes come across as the 'negative outlook brigade', but the reality is that fear of failure or loss can be a powerful motivator. Think about those school or university exam preparations. And remember how the energy levels increase when you discovered that there would be some redundancies in your division?

We are all, to a small degree, motivated by the fear of failure. It's a powerful force. It's why we find things like cold calling so difficult. Many people, for example, find it overwhelmingly stressful to ask a member of the opposite sex out on a date. The fear of failing effectively prevents us from attempting things that we should actually feel okay about doing.

Fear of failure can be a powerful and positive agitator when it comes to making us do things that we might otherwise resist. The fear can be overcome, but it takes practice and an acknowledgement that the outcome is rarely as bad as we imagine it might be.

I've made thousands of cold calls during my business life. But only a handful of those calls have resulted in a negative experience. That's a pretty good hit ratio. Most salespeople will likely have similar cold call statistics, yet many are still daunted by

Leaders must **understand** what **messages** are coming up **through the organisation**, rather than **focusing solely** on the **messages** they may be **sending down**.

the thought of making the call.

Grappling with ways to deal with the fear of failure takes time. The advice given to those of us who struggle with a fear of heights is to regularly expose ourselves to the fear. Beating a fear of failure should, I suspect, be no different. Understand the fear, confront it over and over again, and, eventually, you'll get over it. There must be better ways to drive yourself than resorting to something negative.

NO CHOICE DRIVEN

No choice motivation is, to my mind, the most difficult of all. There are people out there who hate their jobs, but because they have young families to feed they believe they have no choice but to get up in the morning and turn up at a job they don't like. In some, but definitely not all, cases they are good people with negative outlooks.

We managers need to sift out the good ones and try to lift their heads a little. I suggest you try asking people these questions:

- What do you like about your job?
- What don't you like?
- Are there other roles in our business that you'd prefer?
- Are there other roles elsewhere that would utilise your expertise and capability that you would like to try?
- What do you think you would need to do to move into one of those roles?
- Would you like us to work with you to develop a plan to pursue those aspirations?

This logical sequence of questions can be applied to a range of situations. They are not just designed to deal with a poor performer or a no choice individual. It's not difficult to develop a list of questions and to sit down with someone and have this kind of discussion. It does, however, take time, effort and a desire to care.

Because of the pressures we managers and leaders face, we often don't allocate the time to tackle these important tasks. But take the time, and every now and then you'll find someone, somewhere in your business who is underperforming and who, with just a little help, can become a valuable contributor.

* * *

As you can see by the discussion above, the variables around people management are many. Managing people can be enormously challenging, but it can also be

You can **get everything** in life **you want**, **if you just help** enough **other people** to **get what they want**.

Zig Ziglar

unbelievably rewarding. Don't ever underestimate your people, their desire to help you to be successful or their need for your support.

There is one more group of people, however, whose numbers are rapidly growing in our workforces. And they take just a little more understanding. We've even given them a label. We call them millennials.

Postscript 1: People — how to get your people engaged

Remember, most people go to work to do the best they can. But they are not as informed as you are about the state of the business, and chances are, they are not completely clear on how their role fits in to the 'grand plan'. Your people will see different things to what you see and they will have a different sense of what the priorities are.

Here are some simple reminders to keep in mind in leading and managing people.

1. Share with your people what you are trying to achieve.
2. Communicate, communicate, communicate.
3. Get their input into planning and objective setting — they will be more informed of what is happening at the coalface than you are. They might also be more willing to set aspirational goals than you are. They will also be more willing to accept aggressive targets if they have had a part in setting them.
4. Get them positively and proactively involved in issues and solutions.
5. Let them know the outcomes — tell them how you are getting on against the objectives you have collectively set.
6. Work out a way to communicate financial performance without compromising your need for confidentiality. (Note: Sometimes it's better to tell them the whole story.)
7. Reward them for achieving outcomes.
8. Ensure that they have the information to understand the reasons for decisions — particularly difficult decisions.
9. MBWA — walk around, talk to them, understand what their issues are, and be available to help them.
10. Make sure they know that you care about them.

Postscript 2: People — how to conduct more effective performance reviews

I absolutely believe in performance reviews. In my experience, taking the opportunity to sit down with each of the people in your team, one on one, at least once and preferably twice a year, is a 'must do' for managers. What needs to change, however, is what we do once we get into the meeting room. There is no doubt that we need to talk to our people about the role they play in the business and how they are doing. But we also need to listen to what they say about us.

The best results come from having a free-flowing discussion with your people about the business, their role in it, and how we can improve.

As part of any review, you need to give each person some relevant feedback about your views of him or her. People need a combination of positive praise and constructive feedback about the things they could do better.

Here are some questions to focus on as you prepare for the performance review meeting:

- Are they hitting their performance targets? If not, why not?
- What areas do you think they need to work on?
- Do they behave in a manner that is consistent with the expectations in terms of the culture within the business?
- Do they get on well with their co-workers?
- What do their customers (internal and external) think of them?
- Can you point to things they have done really well?
- Are they 'performance aware'? (In other words, do they know whether they are doing well or not doing well?)

That's the easy bit. Now it is time to sit down with them. The major obstacle to running performance reviews as a relevant two-way conversation is this. Most managers are largely incompetent when it comes to conducting a meaningful one-on-one performance-related conversation with their people. This is partly because many managers are not engaged enough in the day-to-day operations of their people, and because they don't see the value in such activities so don't prepare properly. Simply put, many managers don't have the skills and discipline to do this stuff properly.

But what you get out of the performance review process will directly reflect what you put into it.

Remember, there is nothing that is likely to get people as **engaged** as **asking for**, and **listening to**, **their opinion**.

Don't forget, reviews need to be two-way. As part of the process, you need to ensure that you listen to the thoughts of each of your people in respect of their view of your management approach and their comments about the broader company performance and the things the company does. Your people will always be closer to the customers or other stakeholders than their managers. They will see things that you don't see. So we should be treating the performance review as an opportunity to get that feedback and respond to the issues they are highlighting.

So here are some questions that we managers can ask as conversation starters to get a meaningful, two-way performance review under way:

1. How do you think it's going?
2. What do you feel is going really well for you in your role?
3. Are there any areas where you feel you are struggling?
4. Do you get the support you need to do the best job you can?
5. Are there any areas where you feel you would like better support or a different type of support?
6. Tell me about an experience where things have gone really well.
7. Tell me about an experience where we mucked up.
8. Who do you think was at fault there?
9. Tell me about an experience where you got it wrong and what you learned from that.
10. What would you do differently next time?
11. You are much closer to the customer on a day-to-day basis than me — do you see us doing things as a company that could be done better?
12. Do you feel that you are clear on the aspirations of the business?
13. Do you understand what the company objectives are?
14. Do you see the way we act as being conducive to achieving those goals?
15. What else could we do to be better?
16. Do you see us doing unnecessary things that make life difficult for our people?
17. Do we make it easy enough for our customers to deal with us?
18. What do you see our competitors doing that we should be seeking to replicate or improve upon?
19. What could we do better as a company to help people like you to be more effective in your role?
20. If you owned the company, what would be your three main priorities for change?
21. Do you understand what the company is trying to achieve and how your role fits alongside that?

Open, **honest**, **two-way**, **one-on-one** **performance reviews** with your **boss** should be the **right** of **every person** in the organisation.

22. If everything goes well, what aspirations do you have for your career here?
23. What do you think you need to work on to achieve that?
24. How do you think we can help you with those objectives?

Of course, most of these questions can lead on to another conversation. You can then follow up their answers with questions like:

- What do we do about that?
- How do we improve this?
- Is that really happening?
- Does the customer know about this?
- What do you think we should do?
- Give me your opinion?

How you conduct such sessions will depend on the roles of the team you are reviewing. However, if you do this across your team, you will get great feedback on where each of your team members is at and what they are collectively thinking.

* * *

It's not that **Generation F** are **difficult**.
It's just that **managers don't understand**
how to **manage them**.

CHAPTER 8

Managing Millennials

'Millennials have a complicated relationship with money. They're financially optimistic, yet they feel economically restrained. Compensation matters a lot to millennials — but their jobs are about a lot more than their paychecks.'

How Millennials Want to Work and Live
Gallup, 2016

There's a new generation in our workforce. They've been joining up over the last 10 years. They were born between the early eighties and late nineties, and their numbers are growing rapidly in workplaces around the world. Most of them are under 30 years of age. All of them are under 35. I refer to them as 'Generation F'.

'Generation F'. I thought for a while that I had invented the term. However, I saw an article online that had first appeared in the *Harvard Business Review* in 2014, and I realised that someone had beaten me to it.

Generation F. It doesn't mean something disrespectful that your mind might be racing to. In my interpretation it stands for 'The Facebook Generation'. The sons and daughters of baby-boomers who cut their social networking teeth on Myspace, before graduating to Facebook, Instagram, Snapchat, Twitter and, for business, LinkedIn.

Of all the people that we manage today, this is the group that is the most misunderstood. As logic would have it, they are also the group who are least likely to understand those of us who are managing, or trying to manage, them. The reason is simple. These people think differently, act differently and respond differently to

We say:

'You **don't understand** your **place**.

You seem to **want it all now**.'

almost everything we are likely to ask of them or do with them.

They therefore deserve special mention, or, in this instance, their own chapter.

Members of Generation F are just as likely to be part of our own teams as they are to be our customers. There are a lot of them. Currently, they comprise almost 40% of the workforce. By 2025, that number will be approaching 75%. If they like us, they can provide the most wonderful endorsement. If they don't like us, they can kill our business in 24 hours. They are variously described by older generations as selfish, distracted, self-absorbed, early adopters, and 'smartphone jockeys'. Most commonly, they are described as having an unjustified sense of entitlement.

This collective of young people are our future leaders and managers. Some of the better ones are already managing people, and are doing it well.

During my conference presentations, I often ask the assembled audience the following questions:

- *'How many of you work with people under the age of 35?'*
- *'How many of you have clients who are under 35?'*
- *'What do we know about people who are under the age of 35?'*

Those few questions are usually enough to get quite a conversation going. Having quickly ascertained that most of us have colleagues and customers who are members of the Facebook Generation, I then listen to the answers to the last question. Typically the feedback goes something like this:

- *they have a short attention span;*
- *they want instant gratification;*
- *they have a sense of entitlement;*
- *they are technologically savvy;*
- *they are always looking at their phone;*
- *they lack interpersonal skills;*
- *they are idealists;*
- *they like instant information;*
- *they lack focus;*
- *they question everything;*
- *they sulk if they don't get their own way;*
- *you can't tell them anything;*

They say:
'You **don't understand us**.
We are **adaptable**, **accepting** of **change**,
and we know how to **solve problems**.'

- *it's all about them;*

. . . and so on.

For many years now, I have hosted sessions with groups of young leaders, both volunteers and executives. These discussions have often been through my own voluntary work in the form of 'Future Leader' retreats and voluntary forums such as Rotary International's excellent Youth Leader Programme. These sessions are unique in that they attract an audience comprising bright, active young people who are often already inspiring others within their communities.

More recently I have extended this activity into the corporate arena, where we run sessions with future leaders from Gen F to help an organisation's leaders to understand what their people are thinking and how well the 'corporate' messages are being received by this unique group of young people. Thereafter we help the organisation to design better ways of communicating with their younger people.

With a room full of millennials, I ask them a similar question:

- *'What can you tell my generation about people under the age of 35?'*

As you might guess, the answers this time around are very different. They typically include:

- *we embrace things;*
- *we are very accepting of change because it is all we have ever known;*
- *we are adaptable;*
- *we are information hungry;*
- *we acknowledge, understand and are accepting of cultural differences;*
- *we are good at multi-tasking;*
- *we are problem solvers;*
- *we are not constrained by traditional thinking;*
- *we are therefore bold and open-minded;*
- *we know how to use tools to get information and answers quickly;*

. . . you get the idea.

The interesting thing about their responses is that they could fill the next three

Our parents' generation went to the most brutal of wars or saw its impact when troops returned home (or didn't).

Our generation was independent. We walked to school, sat on the back of tractors or utes, and climbed trees when no one was looking.

When we were hurt, and broken bones were not uncommon, we had to work out how to deal with it, often limping home before sundown to get ointment or a bandage or both.

By contrast, Generation F have always been discouraged from taking risks. And even so, if something goes wrong, we make sure they have a cellphone so they can call us for help.

So, don't be surprised by what you see in Generation F.
What you see is our fault.

pages of this book. Gen F have lots of ideas about what they are good at. The other interesting thing about the Gen F answers is that they are largely correct. This is a very 'self-aware' generation.

Of course, this isn't the first time in history that different generations have had trouble understanding each other. In fact, disagreements about the propensity of the younger generation to make a meaningful contribution to society have raged for as long as I can remember and go back as far as my grandparents' generation at least, and probably beyond.

However, I am willing to suggest that this current generation is the most misunderstood, and probably the most well meaning, of them all.

Yes. There is no question that the members of Gen F are demanding. They want to understand how things work and why. They are more confident about asking questions, and they have grown up to expect answers. They want to know why their job is important and how they fit into the overall scheme of things. They are desperate to be accepted and to feel that they are valued.

And, do you want to know why they are so demanding? Because we created them. We shouldn't be surprised by this. I have heard many people describe today's university graduates as the 'needy generation'. While that may be true, much of the blame for this neediness must sit with their parents, a group that I call (with tongue firmly planted in my cheek, because I am one of them) 'Generation H'. You see, the great majority of those of us who are in our forties and fifties are the first ever 'helicopter parents' generation.

Not only did these kids grow up hearing nonsense like 'participation is more important than winning' and 'you can have anything you want'. They have also been fussed over every step of the way.

Our generation of baby-boomers walked to school, or travelled by bus, or in some cases rode our bikes. Whichever mode of transport we were forced to take, we were independent. A generation later and the universal arrival of the two-car family, which coincided with increased concerns about the security of children in the late 1980s and 1990s, resulted in many of today's millennials travelling to school by car. As a former school chairman, I can also assure you that many of those parents then walked their child from the car park to the classroom.

We grew up being told that 'children should be seen and not heard'. When we asked a question, we were often told that we 'didn't need to know about that'.

By contrast, today's young people have grown up in an environment surrounded by correctness, with adults — parents, teachers and caregivers alike — bending over backwards to answer their every query.

They are **not** as **resilient as us**.
They have **grown up differently**.
They have had **more direction**
and **support**.
They have had **unprecedented access**
to information.
We **can't expect them** to get a job and
instantly **start behaving like we do**.

As a result, they have always felt involved. They have always had someone fussing over them. Talking to them. Listening to them. Correcting them and giving them feedback. They have been rewarded for wanting to know the answers, rather than being pushed aside. So it should be no surprise that they want the same ability to have conversations, present their views and ideas, challenge the status quo, and get feedback, at work.

In parallel, while those young people have been growing up, the huge surge in the enablement of technology has supported their 'need to know' and they have become adept at finding the answers to anything they want to know. They can connect with or follow people they aspire to learn from or to be like. In fact, as we know, Gen F are forever online and permanently engaged at every level in nearly everything that is going on in their lives.

If they have friends overseas, they check in with them several times a day. They know where each other are, who they're with and what they're doing. They can organise a night out for 20 people with a 15-second message. Instant. Such a plan would have taken the 20-year-old me 20 phone calls from the land line in my parents' kitchen, or, worse, an invitation sent out by mail, 10 days earlier. They look at the photos from such nights out within seconds of them being taken. Instant. Our photos took a week to get developed. What's more, they comment and contribute to the ensuing discussion, even from the other side of the world. If they're athletes, they know who their key competitors are, when they're training and whether they are injured. If they are musicians or actors, they can rehearse online and audition by Skype from their own bedroom for a role that's 8000 kilometres away.

When it comes to job hunting, they help each other and they can help you. A well-connected '20-something' is probably better placed to quickly find you a new receptionist or a replacement warehouse worker than any number of well-meaning recruitment firms. In fact, for all of the negative things said by my generation about Generation F, my experience suggests that the positives outweigh them tenfold.

In fact, the only area of their lives where they are not permanently engaged is at . . . WORK!

Imagine what happens when young people who grow up in the supportive environment outlined above suddenly arrive at their new workplace where:

- no one tells them what the company does;
- the boss doesn't speak to them when he or she walks past — often multiple times a day;
- they are actively discouraged from speaking to some people;

The only area of their lives where they are **not permanently engaged** is at . . .

WORK!

- they don't understand how they are meant to contribute to the enterprise;
- they are given meaningless roles.

Is it any wonder that they lose interest quickly?

The world's business researchers have identified this issue and their commentaries give us some clues as to what tomorrow's leaders are looking for today.

Gallup, the USA-based analytics and advisory firm, conducts regular research around personnel engagement within organisations. Gallup's 2016 report entitled 'How Millennials Want to Work and Live' shared some of the following findings about the millennial generations:

- just 29% of millennials are engaged in their jobs;
- only 50% plan to remain with their current employer for the next 12 months and yet 60% are open to looking at other opportunities;
- just 19% of millennials in jobs receive regular feedback about their performance.

HR consulting firm Hudson added the following:

- 13% of new hires left their job within three months, mainly because of the organisation's culture (30%) or their manager (36%).

LinkedIn's annual Talent Trends survey talked about prospective candidates looking at new roles, where their primary interest was:

- culture and values (80% of candidates);
- the leadership of the company (63%).

Despite the long list of positives that millennials can bring to business, some of this information implies that they are difficult to attract and engage, and they come with a high risk of early attrition.

For all of their digital connectedness, they remain largely professionally disengaged.

Part of the reason is this. Notwithstanding the exterior bravado and capability, a lot of them lack confidence. Many of them started working before, during or immediately after the GFC. Job losses have been a constant reality during their work lives. Many of their friends remain unemployed, and have never had the job they

A number of '**likes**'
on a **Facebook post** provides a
superficial 'pat on the back'
from a **distant community**.

thought they had prepared themselves for, despite their university qualifications. They are quite demanding of themselves and yet their expectations are low. As one of them told me during a Generation F roundtable session, 'We have gone from "You can do anything" to "You should do everything".' My own view is that many millennials are struggling to work out where they fit.

Many also carry student debt.

For solace, they go to their smartphone where information and gratification is only a swipe away; where they can communicate and be 'liked' as required. Many in Generation F are not good at face-to-face communication, at building meaningful relationships, or at having real conversations. In their eyes, a series of text messages can mean they are 'talking to' someone. A number of 'likes' on a Facebook post provides a superficial 'pat on the back' from a distant community.

I talk to these people regularly. The friends of my daughter and my son just happen to be Gen F. My daughter's friends have mostly graduated from university and are in their first or second real jobs. My son's mates are working part time while they finish school and start university. Let me tell you what they think about how they are treated at work. They say it 'sucks'. (Their language, not mine.)

As leaders and managers, we have this wonderful opportunity to harness the talent, however, at the same time, we must work with our millennials to help them to build their confidence and fully develop the skills and capability for the real world in which they are now required to participate.

Let's now imagine that you have Generation F in your customer base. What do you think these people who are permanently engaged in every aspect of their lives are thinking if you don't return their phone call from yesterday afternoon? Or you don't get the new product pricing to them when you promised?

If you are as responsive and engaging as Generation F expects, they will be loyal and supportive. If you are not, and you 'leave them hanging' (again, their terminology, not mine), then they will make a comment to their thousands of friends about how you let them down and quickly move on.

Harnessing the connections and engagement levels of Gen F is the single biggest people management and customer opportunity out there today. In fact, I'll go a step further. If our generation doesn't work out how to proactively manage and support the Facebook Generation, then they will end up managing us. And they'll be better at it too. Because they are organised, disciplined and connected, they follow up, and they know how to get things done.

In fact, they are brutal about following up because, as noted earlier, they can't stand being uninformed.

Just **29% of millennials** are **engaged** in their **jobs**. But give them **information**, **scope**, **involvement** and **permission** to enable them to **engage themselves**, and **see what happens**.

So, how do you meet the expectations of these people in order to get them as engaged at work as they are in other areas of their lives? It might relieve you to know that I am not saying that we have to send them a text message every three minutes or comment on their Facebook wall every couple of hours.

However, we do have to give them the information, scope, involvement and permission to enable them to engage themselves. That goes back to some of the things we've already discussed.

While we may think that Gen F are demanding, what's interesting is that responding to those demands is relatively straightforward. In fact, if we give them good basic leadership, the nature of which I have discussed throughout this book, they will be highly responsive. Based on my experiences, here are some ideas about the things they want:

1. They want to know what the company is about. What are the organisation's values, and what is the leadership trying to achieve? Where is the business going and what does the future look like? What are the key strategic objectives. Who are the key people? Who are the important customers?
2. They want to know how their role fits into those objectives, and they need to clearly understand what is expected of them. These people are desperate to contribute and they want to know why their role is important.
3. They want their role to be meaningful and relevant. Don't hire a university graduate and ask them to make coffee and collect your dry-cleaning. They want a real job and they want to be able to understand why their job matters.
4. They are keen to know how the organisation as a whole is performing. These people can't stand not knowing what's going on. Tell them what the business is doing well and where there is a need for improvement. Give them financial performance information if you can. They want to know that they are part of a successful organisation.
5. They want feedback and lots of it. Are they doing a good job? If so, tell them. If not, tell them. And don't wait until the annual performance review. Make sure that any negative feedback is immediate, current, specific, relevant, fair and constructive. If it's just general, negative feedback, or you're berating them for something that happened some time ago, they won't understand, and in fact will assume, often incorrectly, that you are carrying a grudge and that you don't like them. As one young leader working for one of the big banks said to me recently, **'You have to remember that we grew up getting gold stars on our homework.'**

Make sure that any **negative feedback** is **immediate**, **current**, **specific**, **relevant**, **fair** and **constructive**.

6. They will tell you that they are good at handling change because they have grown up in a rapidly changing society. However, they are quite resistant to change if they don't understand the reasons for it. So, by all means involve them in the transformation projects, but make sure they understand why you are doing it.

7. They want to be involved. Don't tell them what to do. Rather, include them in the conversation and encourage them to help to identify what needs to be done. If they are part of the decision-making process, their enthusiasm for the task will increase disproportionately, you will get greater engagement and a better outcome.

8. They want their opinion to matter. Listen to them. They will feel that they have ideas that are relevant to the business challenges and they will want to be able to share these. Remember they are used to people listening to their opinions.

9. Make sure you give them the tools they need to do the job. After all, they have always had the tools. Gen F are also the smartphone generation and they have always had the latest iPhones and Apple laptops at high school. If you give them a clunky two-year-old Lenovo ThinkPad on their first day, don't expect them to be grateful. They will probably just bring their own computer to work.

10. Finally, they want to understand what the future looks like. This is not a generation that is scared of change; they will embrace it, as long as they understand what it looks like. They are keen to understand what the future looks like for the organisation, but also for themselves. They are ambitious and they want to know that they will progress and do new things if they do a good job. They like to know that they are making progress, at least at the same rate as their peers. If not, they need to understand why. (Back to the feedback factor again.)

At the risk of repeating myself:

Clarity of purpose. Communication. Consistency.

Gen F wants to understand what the business is trying to achieve and how that relates to what they have to do. They need to know why they are doing things. They are more desperate for success than our generation ever was. But they want to believe in your story, and they will feel let down if you don't deliver. Properly informed, they will be supportive of the organisation's objectives, and they will do their best to engage their substantial networks to help you achieve them.

These people who are **permanently engaged** in **every aspect of their lives can't stand not knowing stuff.** They are **not being rude.** They just want to **know what's going on.** **Communicate** with them and they will **reward you.**

I like Generation F. They are bright, articulate, educated and interested. They can find stuff quicker and more accurately than we can. And they're focused. They follow up. They return calls. They send out marketing information or customer follow-ups when they are due to happen. Properly trained, they will ask the right questions about why you lost a piece of business or where you might go for a referral or a new client. The reason is simple. They can't stand not knowing stuff and they expect to know everything that's going on around them.

There's something else about our young people that is seldom spoken about. They have an innate sense of fairness. Fairness is a big issue for the millennials I interact with. They have grown up in a politically correct environment, where diversity has been more acceptable and rights of the individual more respected. That means that they will be more accepting of negative feedback if it seems fair. They are interested in their remuneration relative to their peers, not only because they are competitive, but also because they want to be sure that they are being treated fairly.

In a funny sort of way, the Facebook Generation don't want anything that is over and above what the generations of workers before them wanted or deserved. It's just that those generations were not equipped to ask for information or to expect to be listened to. Members of Generation F have had full information and total engagement at every level and at every stage of their young lives. They can't cope without it. And they feel comfortable expecting it.

The generations before them never had information or permission. They would have liked it, but were used to coping without it. So what does Generation F really want? When you think about it, it shouldn't be that difficult. In fact, it should be the things we do for all of our people.

In other words, all of our people, irrespective of the generation they come from, deserve to understand what the organisation is trying to achieve, who the key people are, what's important, and how their role assimilates with the key objectives of the organisation. We should all have our opinions considered by those making the decisions, and we all want feedback — the good and the bad. As I have said elsewhere, the reality is that the great majority of people go to work with the intention of doing a good job. Perhaps Gen F are really just the first generation who have had the audacity to draw this to the attention of their managers.

Postscript 1: 10 messages from millennials to their managers

1. What is the organisation trying to achieve?
2. Tell me who our key people are and how I can interact with them.
3. How does my role fit into the overall plan — how do I contribute to the achievement of the company objectives?
4. Make my role meaningful and relevant.
5. Please give me current, regular, constructive feedback and help me to grow.
6. How do I know if I am being successful?
7. Talk to me and listen to my opinions and ideas, and don't criticise me for asking dumb questions.
8. Help me to understand why we are doing the things that we do.
9. Give me the tools I need to do the job.
10. Tell me where we are heading and help me to understand what the future looks like for our business and my role in that.

Postscript 2: 10 messages from managers to millennials

1. Listen to experienced people. They are not old, or out of date. They are experienced and you can learn from them.
2. Understand the differences between the way you were brought up and the real world; you won't always win and you are not always right.
3. You have to prove yourself before you will get promoted.
4. Sometimes you will have to do stuff you don't want to do, but you will learn a lot from those experiences.
5. Keep asking good questions. You will learn much as a result. If that frustrates your boss, you are at the wrong place.
6. Work really hard to have meaningful conversations with other people — face to face. Yes, even people you don't know well.
7. The ability to build and maintain strong relationships with your team and your customers will always be important — and you don't build relationships via social media. Be face to face as often as possible.
8. If you are not getting recognised or making an impact within six months, that's okay. Learn the business, develop your skills, try different things and grow your role gradually as your skills develop.
9. Make the most of every opportunity, especially if you are given the opportunity to lead — take it.
10. Put your phone away. Look for opportunities to talk to people rather than stare at your phone — in the coffee shop or in the meeting room. Offer to help others instead of checking your Instagram feed. This will not come naturally to you. But it will help you to develop a broader range of people skills and you will build better relationships.

I think it is possible for **ordinary people**

to **choose** to be **extraordinary**.

Elon Musk
Founder PayPal, Tesla
and SpaceX

CHAPTER 9

Leading You, Leading Me

'Tomorrow is the most important thing in life. Comes into us at midnight very clean. It's perfect when it arrives and it puts itself in our hands. It hopes we've learned something from yesterday.'

John Wayne
Actor

In these pages, I have spent a lot of time discussing the needs of the business, the people you work with and, to a lesser extent, the customers who make it all possible. But there is one group of people that I have ignored to this point, and they are often the loneliest people in the organisation. They carry the responsibility and the pressure. They must deal with the reality of yesterday and the potential of tomorrow. They must often do so while others (directors, bankers, family members, former employees, and now numerous observers via social media) who are less involved and substantially less informed present them with opinions as to how things should be done.

Of course I refer to you. Me. The manager. The leader. The boss. The loneliest person in the room. Douglas Hitchcock was my first real workplace mentor of any note. His colourful and entrepreneurial business background, and his willingness to share his stories and experiences, have left me and countless others with a lifetime of business lessons. A former Fletchers executive, Doug founded and developed Realty Brokers, a company he later invited me to lead. I learned an enormous amount from him over many years, before, during and after working for him. He's 85 years old now, and remains as sharp as a tack, and a source of inspiration.

Are you

a **remote leader** or

an **involved leader?**

Not sure?

Ask your people.

Of the many things I learned from Doug, the following messages resonate almost daily:

1. Make sure you understand the detail, so other people can't pull the wool over your eyes.
2. Make the most of your available time, and always be 'at the line' (meaning 'up to date').
3. Don't forget to go home to your family.

Valuable advice for any of us.

Detail: Sweating the small stuff

There are, as those of us who've experienced working for someone know, countless approaches to leadership and almost as many leadership styles as there are leaders who practise them. Some of us will have experienced working with leaders who are fantastic, while others we've experienced should never have been put in the positions they occupy.

I am often intrigued by the two extremes in terms of leadership style. These extremes are what I call the 'remote' and the 'involved' leader.

The remote leader occupies his or her role while remaining quite distant; sitting upstairs, in his or her office, focusing on strategy and leaving the day-to-day execution of things to others. We've all seen examples of the remote CEO. At its worst, if you've read American author and former debt trader Larry McDonald's book *A Colossal Failure of Common Sense*, in which he eloquently and shockingly explains Lehman Brothers role in the global financial crisis, you'll know what I mean. McDonald's portrayal of the Lehman Brothers senior executive team in the midst of the crisis is a case study on how the remote leader can fail his or her organisation, people and customers.

Being a hands-on CEO or an involved leader can get on people's nerves sometimes. The reason is you sometimes get in the way, you ask a lot of questions, and you challenge the decision-making. People sometimes misinterpret your desire to stay close to things as a lack of confidence in the role they are performing. But the reality is the opposite. Those activities keep you informed and ultimately make you and your team much more effective. The closer you are to the action, the more likely you can support your people as they go through awkward discussions and difficult decisions.

Undercover Boss . . . what a joke. A TV programme about bad bosses who don't do their jobs properly, who put on disguises and talk to their people, and try to understand what is going on in their business . . . all glamorised by a TV crew following them around.

These bosses should be fired.

The involved, or hands-on, leader operates at the opposite extreme from the remote manger. He or she is the leader who makes sure all the strategic direction and vision stuff happens while remaining deeply involved in the execution and day-to-day operations of the business.

A hands-on leader gets involved at a relatively detailed level with as many relevant aspects of the business as possible. As noted above, it means that you sometimes get in the way of your team members. This perceived negative is, I believe, well and truly outweighed by the positive of knowing what's going on throughout your business.

Above everything else, leaders must be accessible and visible to their people and often their customers. This is particularly the case as more and more of our people belong to the Facebook Generation. To illustrate what I mean, consider the following example:

I recently undertook some consultancy work for a large Australian organisation. One of the company's divisions comprised about 2000 people. The CEO of this particular business used to catch the goods lift to his eleventh-floor office, so as to avoid bumping into his people. To me, that's just plain daft. You have to enjoy getting into an elevator with members of your team. It's an opportunity. You see how people interact. You hear them talking. You can judge by their behaviour and body language how they feel about you.

So now we have reality television programmes, like *Undercover Boss*, which seek to glamorise senior executives who don disguises and go out into the field with their people. These business managers should be doing the rounds of their people as a matter of course, rather than disguising themselves and attempting to integrate with their people because a TV crew is following them around.

And guess what? On those same stupid TV programmes the 'boss' is invariably surprised by some of the behaviours they find going on in their own businesses.

Hello? The problem is not with the people exhibiting the behaviours at the 'factory floor'. The problem is with those bosses who are having their 15 minutes of celebrity fame, who otherwise don't understand what is going on inside their businesses. They are made to look more stupid and more inadequate than they are. Those same bosses are the ones who should be fired by their boards.

Conversely, when I was growing up, my father, who spent many years running large grocery warehouses for Foodstuffs, New Zealand's largest grocery wholesaler, influenced my approach to leadership. These were big operations

Understand the **detail**.

It gives you an **unfair advantage**.

with warehousing, self-service retail, inwards goods, trucks in and trucks out. In those days, most product was handled manually, and he was always kind enough to ensure that I, and some of my friends, had guaranteed work in the warehouses during most of our school and university holidays.

Long before In Search of Excellence and MBWA, I always noticed the first thing Dad did each day. The doors opened at 8 a.m., and at 7.55 a.m. every morning he would leave his office and 'walk the floor', from one end of the enormous building to the other. He did so under the pretence of saying good morning to all of his people, which he did as he went. But, in reality, as he explained to my younger self, he was doing much more.

This simple act of walking the floor and greeting every member of the team at the start of his day gave him the opportunity to observe the state of the facility and the presence of his team. As he wandered, he took note of who was at work on time, and who wasn't. He would always notice whether the battery-operated forklifts had been properly stored and charged overnight. A rogue pallet that hadn't been put away would always attract his attention, as would yesterday's 'spill' that hadn't been cleaned up properly. And he was able to develop a daily sense of the status of the orders coming in and those waiting to depart. Were there orders stacked up in the aisles waiting to be sent out? Had yesterday's inwards goods been put away? Was the warehouse clean and tidy?

The flipside, of course, was that his people knew he would be walking around every morning. They knew to expect him. So the operation was always in pretty good shape. Because he spoke to every one of them most mornings, members of his team felt that they knew him well enough to approach him for a discussion.

They would approach him with questions about the computer system or difficulties with certain suppliers or customers.

He was constantly talking to a forklift driver, a shelf stacker or a checkout operator. Did he get in the way of his team of managers? No way. To the contrary, he was able to be very supportive of them because he knew what was going on in his business. He would cover thousands of square metres of warehouse every morning. And by 8.30 a.m. every day, he knew exactly what was going on in his business.

In the era before computer systems enabled us to know the status of our businesses by the minute, he was teaching me how to do so the old-fashioned way. Tom Peters and Hewlett-Packard would have called that MBWA.

Visible

+

Accessible

=

Approachable

Of course, by contrast, most of today's managers arrive at work and go straight to the email screen. At the risk of stating the obvious, you don't see what's going on in your business while you are staring at your computer screen.

Being visible and accessible offers a two-way benefit. Your people see you and you are more approachable as a result. But you also see them and you get to observe your business in everyday operational mode. What's going on, what's working and where the problems are. Think Undercover Boss without the disguises and TV cameras. If you are out there, your people will make use of you. Think about the techniques and ideas earlier in this book, and my earlier comments about communication and MBWA. Some of the activities suggested such as walking the floor, sitting in open plan, morning teas and big room meetings, will all serve to enable you to develop a leadership style that is involved and participative, and that works.

It works because you are putting yourself in a position to form your own views about what is going on in the business, rather than relying on the perceptions of others.

* * *

My life now as a professional director, business advisor and speaker means I watch, carefully, how other leaders and managers work. I greatly admire some business leaders. Others, less so.

I've been fortunate to get to know or to witness some fantastic examples of outstanding leaders who have been just that — involved. In almost every case, their attention to what others would regard as immaterial details has been among the things to set them apart. Here are some examples:

Back in 2006, my wife, Rose, and I were guests at the Virgin Ball, hosted by **Sir Richard Branson** at his airline's hangar at Brisbane Airport. Because we were on airport property, the security process was full on and slow going. We were taken by bus from our hotel to the secret venue and, upon arrival, joined a very long queue for what seemed like an extremely long wait.

> *Being on airport property in the post 11 September 2001 environment, our evening started with a walk through a couple of metal detectors, much as you do when boarding a flight. But in this case, we were some three thousand people dressed in our ballroom best, complete with, in the case of the ladies present, various items of jewellery. You can imagine how long it took for each couple to*

If you don't **try** to **make a difference** in the **world**, you've **wasted your life**.

Sir Richard Branson
Founder Virgin Group
Auckland, 2017

get through the security checkpoint.

So, where was Sir Richard while all this was going on? He was walking up and down the queue, introducing himself to his guests and saying things like 'Hi, I'm Richard. Thanks for coming. Sorry about the security, but you've got to do it nowadays.'

He stayed in the line for about 90 minutes, working the crowd, introducing himself and asking his guests to introduce themselves before we went in to enjoy his hospitality. He didn't leave until the queue had subsided and only then did he join the party inside.

I watched him throughout the evening as he engaged with his guests non-stop. Towards the end of the evening, Rose and I had quite a chat to him. He was every bit as focused and engaged as he was at the start of the evening, even making sure I knew what we had to do to support his business.

Do you think he's in touch with the people interacting with his businesses? Absolutely he is.

∗ ∗ ∗

I always enjoyed any involvement I had with my old boss, the late **Kerry Packer**. Packer was an Australian business legend and rightly so. By the time I arrived at his Publishing and Broadcasting Limited (PBL) empire, he was in his sixties and his lifetime of ill health had taken its toll. When it came to the social scene, he was no Richard Branson. But he had the same attention to detail, albeit with a different focus.

I bumped into him in the lift during one of my visits to Sydney. There were about six people in the lift, but for a few moments he only noticed me. Age and ill health notwithstanding, he was still a big man. He was tall and erect and his hands were the size of dinner plates. Having just posted another record profit, I might have hoped for a better reception than I received. 'What the hell are you doing over here?' he asked.

To put his next comment into perspective, the New Zealand magazine business for which I was responsible at the time comprised 55 titles and published 116 issues per month. In Australia, the PBL business comprised the then leading free-to-air TV channel, Channel 9, the Crown Casino hotel and gambling operation, ACP Magazines with over 200 publications per month

You **don't see** what's **going on in your business** while you are **staring** at your **computer screen**.

in Australia, plus a dozen or so in Asia. And then there were the various Packer family investment interests including, among other things, Australia's largest farming operations with thousands of acres of livestock in New South Wales, Western Australia and the Northern Territory.

'Why the heck did you put that tart on the cover of Cleo?' he asked, referring to the latest cover story on one of our magazines. 'Don't you know she doesn't sell magazines?' he added. 'That image didn't sell in Australia last month and it won't sell over there.'

I admit, I was still trying to recall who we had on the cover of Cleo that month when the door opened at his level 2 office and his large frame stepped out of my sight as rapidly as it had imposed itself on me, two floors earlier. Like Branson and my father before him, but in a very different way, Packer was letting me know that he was in touch with what was going on. His capacity for understanding and recalling detail was fascinating.

* * *

Until its demise in recent years, APN News & Media was one of Australasia's largest print media companies. Their printing capacity made them one of ACP's most important suppliers. During my time in the magazine business we were APN's largest printing client. APN was New Zealand's biggest media company and a subsidiary of the Irish-based Independent News & Media, then ultimately owned and controlled by Irish businessman **Sir Anthony O'Reilly**. Like Branson and Packer, O'Reilly had his uniqueness, which stamped him as an outstanding and involved leader.

Tony O'Reilly was, in his day, an outstanding sportsman who represented Ireland and the British Lions at rugby union. He was one of the stars of the Lions team that toured New Zealand in 1959 when, in his own words, he fell in love with our country. Some 30 years later he began eyeing our rugby-mad nation as an investment destination. As CEO of US food giant Heinz, he bought our local food company, Wattie Industries, and soon after added the country's largest media organisation to his personal portfolio.

Sir Anthony would, during his frequent visits to New Zealand, entertain clients and key contacts of the APN Group over dinner, either individually or in groups of 12 or so. I was fortunate enough to be invited to both kinds of encounter.

Branson and Packer both focused on the detail, but what struck me most about O'Reilly was his preparation. He was always incredibly well briefed. I imagined

It's always **easier** for **someone to ignore you**, or be **disrespectful**, if they **don't know you**.

And **vice versa**.

So **get out** and **make sure** that **you know the people** and **they know you**.

he must have had a team force-feeding him information about his guests, their names and their businesses, and how they related to APN's wellbeing.

His preparation, coupled with his wonderful Irish raconteur style, made him easy to like. And although I met him only a few times, I was always left with the impression that he knew who we were and that he regarded us as important clients. He was always up to date with any current issues and I knew that I could call him should I ever need to.

On the odd occasion that I felt the need to do just that, he was exactly what I had expected. Informed, understanding and solution focused.

✳ ✳ ✳

Involved leaders bring the distinct advantage of being closer to every aspect of the detail of their business. They're seen around the factory floor or the sales offices and thereby get to know their people. They are therefore seen as being more approachable and in touch. Most importantly, involved leaders see and understand what's going on at the coalface. As a result, they understand the impact of the decisions they make.

The involved leader makes an organisation more effective. He or she also changes the culture of an enterprise by their actions. If people think the CEO might drop by, they're more likely to be focusing on doing the right job right. That's partly because they don't want to get caught out and partly because they believe that the leader cares about and understands the importance of what people in various parts of the business are doing.

Think about it. It's always easier for people to be disrespectful to those that they don't know. The involved leader gets to know their people and makes them feel more important than perhaps they think they are. In turn, your people are more respectful of you and the role that you occupy, and they are more motivated to do a better job.

It is not, of course, just international billionaires whose attention to detail and closeness to the customer stamps them as unique. There are wonderful examples of 'hands on' leadership in many organisations. Sadly, there are plenty of examples of 'hands off' leadership as well.

I regularly hear people saying 'Don't sweat the small stuff', and yet what these billionaires show us by standing in line or remembering our name is how big an impact you can make by bringing the most focused attention to the tiniest detail. So go ahead. Sweat the small stuff. Get the detail right. Walk the floor. Get involved.

Time management:
the **best-kept secret** of the **rich**.

Anon

Time: Maximising the minutes

Somebody once described time management as 'the best-kept secret of the rich'. I don't know if it is or not, but as a young man at the time, it certainly got my attention. This is not a book, or even a chapter, on time management, and it is certainly not intended to be a complete examination of the topic.

However, over the years I have probably had every type of distraction and interruption known to man, threatening to push me off course at one time or another.

As the leader, everyone wants a piece of you. It is very easy to spend 100% of your time talking to your people about whatever might be important to them. While some interruptions are to be welcomed, because they mean you are getting involved in the important stuff, unplanned interruptions can also be your enemy, especially if they are too frequent, too long or the reason for them is not relevant.

Yes, it's great to stand by the water cooler and chat to your people about the weekend weather, the holiday shopping or the test match results. You build rapport doing that. But keep it limited, keep moving and manage the amount of time you spend tightly.

We have to understand that there are going to be times when your people, bosses or customers need to talk to you and that conversation has not been planned. But we all need a few techniques to help us avoid those days where we are staring at the daily action list at 6 p.m. with nothing ticked off.

If you watch the most well-organised people, you will note that they all use tools and disciplines to keep them on track. Without those support structures, we all tend to drift and sometimes miss what's important. The higher the level of personal organisation, the better the likelihood that we will drive our own productivity.

Here are some of the lessons that I've learned along the way.

CREATE AN ACTION LIST — EVERY DAY

A list of things to do must be the oldest time management tool in the world. The best to-do list is old fashioned too: written or printed on a sheet of paper that sits, permanently visible, atop your pad or daily papers. I must have tried every electronic to-do list. The trouble is, as soon as you close your laptop or iPad, your list disappears from view.

As well as being visible, make sure your to-do list is prioritised. I used to use a detailed prioritisation system that gave every single action a place in the daily 'pecking order'. The problem, however, is that your day doesn't run according to A1

Take good notes.

Take notes from every meeting and every conversation.

Write everything in one place — a book or a journal is best. Then you always know where to look for your ideas.

Write your notes on the right-hand side of the double-page spread.

Write your actions on the left-hand side.

That way, it's easy to sit down at the end of the day and summarise the things you have to do.

to E7. Don't over-complicate it; just three simple headings will do for most of us:

- Must do today.
- Must do this week.
- Would like to do sometime.

Review and update your list daily. Make sure that the immediate priorities within your list are rewritten every day. As you write, you will remind your subconscious of what needs to be done. The mere exercise of writing out your list by hand exercises your subconscious in a way that sees you automatically doing things throughout the day without reference to your list. At the end of the day you will look at your list and realise that you have done a number of the important tasks, all without referring to your list.

Finally, when you go back to your desk after a meeting or other event, go to your to-do list first, before looking at your email. That way you ensure that you are always focusing on the most important priorities first.

MAKE MEETINGS WORK

We all spend too much time in meetings. Some of those meetings are a waste of time. In big companies we find people who have made an art form of going to meetings that they don't need to be at, in order to fill an hour or so in their diary. So here are my tips for maximising your presence at meetings.

1. Only have a meeting if you need a meeting. If you can get by with a five-minute chat in the corridor instead, do that.
2. Make sure there is a topic and an agenda.
3. Have an allocated timeframe that is sufficient to deal with the agenda.
4. Start on time.
5. Be clear on what you would like to achieve out of the meeting. Take with you a series of bullet points and share them with the group at the start of the discussion so everyone knows why you're there. Invite participants to add to the list of meeting outcomes as you do so.
6. Ensure that the people you need to have at the meeting to get the targeted outcomes are available and present. If they can't be there, reschedule until you have the right people in the room.
7. Ensure that you don't have people present who don't need to be there. They can go elsewhere and do something productive.

Meetings checklist:

1. Agenda circulated in advance.

2. Ensure that the required people are present.

3. Start on time.

4. Commit to a finish time.

5. Set clear goals for meeting outcomes.

6. Agree next steps on each point.

7. Take good minutes with action points and names of those responsible.

8. Circulate minutes and actions to all attendees within 48 hours.

8. Ask someone to take minutes, and make sure that action points are captured. A meeting without action points is a waste of time.
9. If the meeting is a regular event, go through the minutes of the last meeting at the start and make sure that actions have been followed up. If they haven't been, try to understand why, revisit the actions and reconfirm the importance of having those items completed before the next session.
10. Finish on schedule.
11. Circulate the minutes within 48 hours, while the information and outcomes are still fresh in everyone's minds.

BLOCK OUT TIME

Your second most important instrument in managing your time effectively is your diary. But your diary is not just for appointments. You need to use it to manage your availability for others.

As part of your forward planning, block out chunks of time, at the same time every day or week or month. The best way I know to maximise your effective use of time is to have consistent agendas. For example, depending on the seniority of your role, you will need to block out some planning time. Maybe two hours every two weeks. If you have to travel away from the business regularly, do so on the same day of each week. I used to alternate every week between the state capitals in Australia. I made Tuesdays my travel days. As a result, people knew when I was likely to be out of the office and I was able to maximise the ability to plan my time. If you are a sales manager, chances are you will want to spend time out in the territory with members of your sales team. Again, do it at the same time every week.

So Tuesdays might be your travel days, and Thursday mornings might be the time that you are out in the patch with your salespeople. I also try to stay appointment free after 5 p.m. That allows me to wrap up emails and phone calls between 5.00 p.m. and 6.30 p.m. before finalising my action list for the following day.

DELEGATE

If you're a high achiever, you will find that delegation is hard. Those of us who are control freaks have the same problem. You see, we all believe that we can do the job and we want it done to a standard that only we can deliver. The non-delegators among us believe that they have to do everything themselves in order for it to be done to the right standard.

However, we need to understand the downside of that approach. The problem is that we often don't get it all done. Because we are busy, there is a risk that the

Leaders who try a lot of
different things fail often . . . but they
succeed more often.

action, if left to us, won't be taken on time, or it will be rushed at the last minute, or it won't happen at all. As soon as we understand that, it helps us to position the role of delegation in our own minds.

Ideally, we would like to be able to give six tasks to six different people and have those people complete those tasks to the standard that we ourselves would deliver. But that doesn't happen. Chances are that some or all of those six people won't do as good a job as we think we would have done.

But here's the point about delegation. At least they will get it done.

Simply put, we are often better to have something done, to an adequate standard, on time, and to be able to give the outcome 7/10 for execution, rather than waiting to do it ourselves, at sometime in the future, possibly later than necessary, and giving it 9/10.

The key to successful delegation is to understand the skills of the key people you work with, select actions for people that are best suited to their skills, and to brief them properly on what you need them to do. The better the briefing, the better the execution.

Here's a simple example.

Imagine you need to phone an important client and invite them to a function or an event, and you want the client made to feel special. You might be tempted to make the call yourself. However, you can delegate the task, but in doing so, you need to make sure you tell the person making the call why you are inviting the client, why they are important to the company, and how to position the invitation.

Unless you think about how you delegate the task, you might assign this job by saying something like:

'Hey, Sally, can you please call the people on this list and invite them to the boardroom discussion on Thursday?'

This will result in an impersonal call, from someone the client might not know, and the risk of that client not taking the invitation as seriously as they would have if it came from you.

Instead you can try something like:

'Sally, can you please call these clients and invite them to the boardroom discussion on Thursday. Please make it clear to them that they are really important to the firm and I want them there because, not only do we value

As soon as someone

walks into your office,

STAND UP.

our relationship with them, but we also really benefit from the constructive feedback they give us.'

Now Sally has the information she needs to make the call personal, to make the customer feel important, and to let them know that you are looking forward to their participation. It's a simple example, but it applies to delegation across the board. If the person picking up your tasks is well briefed, and they understand what you want them to do and why it is important, you will get a better outcome.

STAND UP

As the manager you will have a constant stream of people coming to you with all sorts of queries and requests. You have to work out how to deal with that line-up of people in a way that is respectful of them, enables you to respond to the issue or opportunity that they want to talk about, and yet enables you to do it in the optimum time. I'm sure we've all had people come into the office, sit down and proceed to overstay their welcome.

So here are three simple tools that I have used over the years, for dealing with these serial interruptions:

#1. Stand up. As soon as someone walks into your office, or up to your workstation, you should stand up before they can sit down. That way they don't get the chance to get comfortable and talk about the weekend weather or sports results. Now, with you both on your feet, you can jump straight to the issue with a politely worded 'How can I help?' If you can solve the problem with a quick discussion, you can do so there and then, and because you are both on your feet, you can start leading the person back to where they came from in a timeframe that suits you.

#2. Put them off. So what happens when the stand-up interruption happens when you really are too busy to deal with it? Ask if it is urgent. Chances are it isn't as urgent as they will think it is. Tell the person you are in the middle of something and ask if it can wait for 20–30 minutes. Chances are it can. Then invite them back in half an hour, or better still . . .

#3. Go to them. The following response will satisfy most people who come looking for assistance from you: 'Can it wait a few minutes? I am just trying to wrap something up, and then I will come down to your workstation.' Now

Email can **hijack your day**.

So, don't start the day with email.

Start the day with the **most important things** you have to do that day.

When those priorities are dealt with,
prepared for or planned,
check your email.

Email can wait until 11 a.m. most days.

you are in control of time. When you go back to see the person, how long you stay and when you leave are all in your control.

CONTROL THE EMAIL MONSTER

If you don't control the email, it will control you. If you start each day with the email, chances are your prioritised to-do list will get lost in the distractions that follow. To the extent that you can, try to set aside times that you deal with email. There will always be times when urgencies occur, and you have to deal with them. But beyond those instances, try to manage email in a way that doesn't distract you from the real priorities of the day.

When I was in corporate life I was getting over 300 emails per day. Nowadays it's more like 100–200. These are my simple rules:

1. I only 'do' email three times a day. Depending on meeting schedules, those times are around mid-morning, early afternoon and evening. Unless there is an urgent matter that needs attention, I avoid starting the day with email. Most of the people you are corresponding with will be happy with a response within four or five hours. If it's more urgent than that, they should call.
2. Don't read the emails that you are only copied (or cc'd) on straight away. Leave those in a holding pen for a couple of days and flick through them at your leisure. If you are required to respond, someone will bring it to your attention.
3. When you come back to your desk after a meeting, resist the temptation to go straight to email. At first, go to your action list or some project activity.
4. Internet use. Although it's different from email, it happens at the same device. And it's the biggest time-waster in your team today. Be disciplined about internet use at all times. You will keep on top of what most news sites have to offer with two visits per day — morning and night. And unless it is strictly business related, stay away from social media while you are working. Your personal social media activity can happen outside work hours.

The one thing in this life that we can't get more of is time. Be wary of time-wasters and do everything you can to maximise every minute of every day.

Sometimes **family life** can be **difficult**.

If **both partners** are **working** and growing kids are getting busier, it can become **extremely hard for everyone**.

But when it is at its most difficult, **there is something** you must **all remember**.

You're all in the same family.

You're all on the same team.

You are doing this for each other.

Family: Go home

I often wonder about the term 'work-life balance'. It seems to me that the real challenge is getting a 'life' in the rather than the work. Maybe we should simplify and rename it 'life balance'.

Ask most executives or managers what their priorities are and they will likely say something along the following lines:

Priority 1. My family.
Priority 2. The business or job.
Priority 3. Myself.

Of course, it doesn't always work out that way. If I think about the times it has worked for my family, and me, it's been when all three of those considerations are constantly revolving in terms of the priority level. In other words, it's not one thing or another that always sits at the top of the pile. They move around. You can't compartmentalise your life. Sometimes you have to answer a call in the evening and sometimes you have to go to the kids' sports day during work hours.

You have to spend time with the kids, have a night out with your wife or partner, get the management report completed, hire a new person, and go to the gym or for a swim or a bike ride. Sometimes, all in one day.

I feel that this is something I have grappled with all of my business life. The constant guilt that you are doing something when you should be doing something else. I know that it is much worse for those of you who are working mothers than it has ever been for me, and even to this day, with grown-up kids, and being self-employed, it remains a challenge.

A few years back I did an aptitude and personality test. Even after all these years, I still learn things about myself as a result of such exercises. Apparently, I have an extremely high 'orientation to duty'. Put simply, that means that I try very hard — harder than most — to meet my obligations, be on time, to do what I say I will do, be prepared, volunteer for stuff and so on.

On the receipt of that information, a number of things suddenly became clear. Like, why I would fly home from an overseas meeting on a Friday night so I could be home with my young family, when the rest of the meeting participants would stay on in Hong Kong, Singapore or some other exotic location for the weekend. Or why I am always reluctant to leave a project or for that matter a job until I have completed what I went there to do.

Ask the boss **for time off** if you have to.

You have to **try to get to** the **birthdays**, the **swimming** or **athletic sports**, the **school show** and the **weekend activities**.

Don't spend your **weekends** at the golf **course** if your kids have something on that you could be watching or participating in.

Believe me, **they will try harder** if **you are there**.

Part of the solution is setting expectations of those around you. Those people at work know that you have a family and that there are times when they are the priority. Meanwhile, your family knows that sometimes business has to take priority. After all, that's how we pay for the best of family times — holidays.

Someone asked me recently, 'How do you do ocean swims and triathlons, and raise great kids while turning companies around?' I'm not sure if my answer is perfect, and there are probably some behavioural psychologists out there somewhere who will do a better job of answering the question than me. But when I thought about it, I realised that I had developed some unwritten rules over the years. They go like this.

ASK THE BOSS FOR TIME OFF IF YOU HAVE TO

You have to try to get to the birthdays, the swimming or athletic sports, the school show and the weekend activities.

Don't spend your weekends at the golf course if your kids have something on that you could be watching or participating in.

Believe me, they will try harder if you are there.

GO HOME AS SOON AS YOU CAN

Business travel often puts pressure on families and guilt on the traveller. I'm not sure that you ever overcome that but you can minimise it. My approach has always been to go away on business, cram everything I can into the tightest possible timeframe, and go home when I'm finished. As tempting as it may be, I don't like to hang around and play tourist when there is a family to go back to. Spend extra time with them now and do your travelling with them when you can.

To illustrate: New Zealand is about as far away as it's possible to get. However, you can fly out on Sunday night and be in London, showered, suited and ready to go, by 9 a.m. Monday London time. Returning home after the close of business on a Thursday night London time, you can walk into the door of your New Zealand home in the early hours of Saturday morning, just in time for the kids to get up and you all go off to Saturday morning sports.

LEAVE THE OFFICE

Get out of the office at the end of the day and get home in time to see the family before bedtime. If they expect you to be there, it becomes as important for them as it does for you. For me, that has typically meant getting out of the office around 6.30 p.m. or 7 p.m. at the latest. Of course there are exceptions, those times when

Your **kids** will **remember** that you were at the **sports day** or **dance recital** long after **the boss** has **forgotten** that you **weren't at the office**.

you just can't leave, but we must try to keep them to a minimum. If I need to take work home, I prefer that to staying longer at the office.

STAY HOME

Before I was married I used to go to the office on weekends. However, that changed when I had a wife and thereafter a daughter. So ever since then I have made it a habit not to go to the office on weekends. Sure, I take work home, and there have been times when I seem to have spent half the weekend working at home. But at least I've been there. We all want to be part of our family's lives, and the stress between work priorities and family priorities can be hard to manage. But you can only be part of your family's life when you're with them. And chances are, they won't be at your office on the weekend.

LOOK AFTER NUMBER ONE

We all need some 'me time'. Looking after our minds and bodies is important, especially if you want to be able to perform in business and in life. In my case that means exercising. For others, that may mean reading or spending time with friends.

I try to keep a reasonable level of fitness in order to enable me to participate in the ocean swims, triathlons, and the occasional game of golf or tennis that I enjoy.

Some people say that they don't have time to exercise. Others suggest that their partner gets cranky when they want to go and have some 'me time'. Like everything else it's about setting expectations, often with your partner. In my case I'm lucky that I married an athlete who understands the need for exercise and the benefits it brings. But there's a limit. I'm sure if I suggested that I prepare for an ironman while working 60 or 70 hours a week, that support might diminish.

So like everything else it's about balance. In my case that means a couple of swims and bike rides a week, which is enough to stay fit and do all the things that I like to do.

GET TO THE 'BIG' EVENTS

You know the ones. Birthdays are critical. If you have three kids, it's only a couple of hours at the most, three days a year. Then there's swimming sports, speech competitions, the school show or the music recital. Prizegivings are critical.

It feels like a big effort to make it to these. They mostly happen in school time, which is, of course, work time. It will take a couple of hours out of your day. You are meant to be in a meeting. The boss might wonder where you are. BUT . . . your kids will remember that you were there long after the boss has forgotten that you

Try **date nights** with your **partner**.

Lock it in the diary.

When you think about it, it's **more important than** the **sales meeting**.

You just have to **make it a priority**.

weren't. And, alternatively, your children will remember that you weren't there when someone else's parent was.

MAKE TIME FOR YOUR PARTNER, SPOUSE, HUSBAND OR WIFE

There is no doubt that the combination of corporate life and family life puts pressure on relationships. How many times have you heard something along the following lines: 'Once the kids left home, we realised that we didn't have anything in common any more.'

Keep in mind that there will be days when your partner is secretly jealous that you 'escape' each day to go to work. So, if you can, hire a babysitter or a relative to look after the kids while you get away for a long weekend every now and then. Or have a 'date night' every second week, where just the two of you go out and do something together.

Keep in touch with each other and keep some things in common. In my case, we cycle most weekends and compete in the odd ocean-swimming event or multi-sport event together. We team up with others and walk trails or ride mountain bikes through some of the great scenery we have in this part of the world. And we go out, drink wine, eat and talk.

Once you establish life balance in your business and personal lifestyle, it becomes important to share the philosophy with others. Of course the easiest way to manage anything is to set the expectations of those around you. That might mean implementing some simple rules. I always try to remind the people I work with to go home at the end of the day. Despite what the occasional lawyer or investment banker may tell you, it's actually okay to go home at 6 p.m. or 7 p.m. You don't need to be there until midnight to prove that you're working hard. In fact, if you're there until midnight, I would suggest that something is wrong.

We should all set aside some times as sacrosanct. Things like getting home before the kids' bedtime at least three days a week, a date night with your partner once or twice a month, being around on weekends, and, of course, holidays. And don't forget your exercise time. It does take discipline. But you can work a 70-hour week and still do this stuff. And let me assure you that your big long list of the many things that can go wrong if you're not at the office probably won't happen.

Postscript: Family

There's an old saying that goes like this: 'No one ever laid on their deathbed wishing they had spent more time at the office!' And then there's another one: 'Happy wife, happy life.'

Here's something else for you to consider. Just as my parents did for my brother and me, I have spent a lifetime standing on the sidelines at kids' sports. I've also spent plenty of time participating with, refereeing or coaching other people's kids. You only have to watch how much harder a child tries when their parents are watching, to realise how important it is to them that you are there. Try it. You might notice that yourself.

Take care and look after the ones that matter.

We need to **internalise** this
idea of **excellence.**
Not many folks spend a lot of time
trying to be excellent.

Barack Obama

CHAPTER 10

A Question of Leadership

'The quality of a leader cannot be judged by the answers he gives, but by the questions he asks.'

Simon Sinek
Author

There are a lot of questions in this book. That's intentional. They are designed to make you think, but also to guide you and to help you to challenge the status quo as it relates to your management experience. These questions are for you to use as you pursue your own leadership journey.

As a leader it is always important to ask good questions, and plenty of them. You cannot be expected to have all the answers, but your people and your customers will be able to help you . . . if you ask.

In the remaining pages that follow, I have shared lists of questions. There is some repetition from what you have already read earlier. But there are also a lot of questions that haven't appeared elsewhere in these pages. It's not meant to be a definitive list of all the questions you might ever need to ask. But there are plenty of questions to get you started, and to enable you to create conversations within your team that you might otherwise never have.

These questions will help you to challenge the status quo, challenge yourself or liven up a discussion with members of your team. They will enable you to set the scene for a planning meeting or a budget review. They will help you to agitate, clarify and learn.

They are there for you to turn to, as you need them. A place to go to before a

If it's **not profitable**,
and it's **not strategic**,
why are we doing it?

difficult meeting or a challenging presentation. A source of ideas or inspiration to help you to challenge your team.

So use them. Carry them with you. I hope that they can help you to become a better leader.

Change

- Are we achieving everything we want in our business?
- What would we like to change?
- What are the things affecting our business that we cannot control?
- What are the things affecting our business that we can control?
- We are now better at collecting data than ever before. What are we doing with it?
- How do we turn data into insights and information?
- Does the 80/20 rule apply to our business?
- How long since we reviewed the 20% of the revenue that takes up 80% of the effort?
- Should we still be in that business?
- Are we tolerating loss-making businesses?
- If so, do we believe there is a strategic reason for doing so?
- If a part of our business is not strategic and not profitable, should we consider exiting that business?
- What is happening externally in our industry?
- Have we had good conversations about gender diversity in our business?
- Have we had good conversations about racial diversity in our business?
- What are the major issues (if any) affecting our success?
- What are the key changes we are seeing in the next 12 to 36 months?
- Are we keeping up with the changes we are seeing?
- Does changing technology play a part in creating future risks to our business?
- Is there potential for a competitor that we don't see coming in our business? (Think Airbnb, Uber, etc.)
- What are the changes we should be considering right now to support the future needs of the business?
- Who are the people responsible for driving various changes within the business?
- What would you do differently if you owned the business? (Assuming you don't own the business.)
- How are we supporting the people in the business who have an entrepreneurial spirit?
- Are we innovating?

What are my

top 5

business priorities

today?

- When was the last time we created a new product or service line?
- Did it work?
- What will our next one be?
- As a leader, how long has it been since I was part of a discussion about a new product idea or some other innovation for our business?

Leadership

- What are we trying to achieve?
- Do we communicate that well?
- Do I personally act in a manner that is consistent with what I expect of our people?
- Are we successful?
- Are we as profitable as we should be?
- Are we growing?
- Where are the growth opportunities in the next 12 months?
- Are we making noise or music?
- Do our people know what we are trying to achieve?
- If not, how do we expect them to help us achieve our goals?
- When was the last time that I sat down with my team and talked to them about the future of the business?
- What are my top five business priorities today?
- How long since I sat down and talked to (and listened to) everyone in my area of the business in groups of eight or fewer?
- When was the last time we had a planning session within our team?
- Does the leadership team meet monthly to discuss financial performance?
- Do we conduct regular reviews ensuring that initiatives and actions are on track?
- Do we have a regular meeting with the entire team?
- If not, how do we keep our people up to date?
- How does teamwork operate in our business?
- Are we tolerant of each other and do we work together well?
- Where are the good examples of collaboration among the team?
- Can we use those examples to ensure better collaboration on other initiatives?
- In what areas does teamwork work well?
- In what areas do we 'fall over'?
- If we look to other divisions within the businesses on whom we rely, do we understand what their main priorities are and how we fit into their plans?
- What are my three biggest priorities over the next 90 days?

Do we have **open discussions** about our **financial performance?**

- Have we broken our goals down into one-month, three-month and 12-month objectives?
- What type of organisation or team do we want to develop?
- How do our people behave, internally and externally?
- In an ideal world, how do we want our people to behave?
- What sort of working environment do we wish to create?
- How would we describe our company culture?
- Do we have a clear Mission Statement that is understood by our people?
- How long since we conducted a SWOT (ORCS) analysis on our business?
- What are our opportunities, risks, capabilities, and shortfalls?
- Is the boss visible and accessible?
- If not, how do I let him or her know?
- What can I do this week to make an impact on our single biggest issue?

Finance and the back office

- Are our monthly accounts completed as soon as possible after the completion of the month? (No more than 10 days later.)
- Are our annual budgets completed and agreed to by those responsible for achieving them?
- How often do we re-forecast the business?
- Does the year-to-date performance affect our view (positively or negatively) of the likely full-year result?
- Do we have to start making changes to our projections (including cost management) to prepare for a softer year than we planned?
- Do we have our annual accounts audited?
- Do we understand the value in having our annual accounts audited and should we do so?
- Do we have open and regular discussions about our financial performance?
- Do our people know whether we are achieving our financial targets?
- How would we describe our relationship with our bankers?
- If that relationship is not strong enough, what can we do to improve it?
- Whose job is that?
- Do we have a three-year financial aspirations outlook?
- What is our anticipated three-year view?
- Are our capital expenditure proposals accompanied by related incremental revenue projections?
- Are we managing our costs closely?

Do our **salespeople** understand our **products well enough?**

- Who audits the spending on company credit cards?
- Do we really need company credit cards? (The answer is no. Let people pay with their own card and claim expenses — they will be less likely to claim things that they shouldn't.)
- Are our software licences current and legitimate?
- Do we have the right technology solutions for our type of business?
- Can clients interact with us electronically, including ordering, delivery and payment systems?

Products and services

- Why should our customers purchase our product or services?
- What is our unique selling point?
- Is my product or service relevant in the current market?
- Does today's product satisfy tomorrow's customer need?
- If not, what are we doing about developing our products and service offerings for a changed future? (Small to medium-sized professional services firms — accountants, lawyers, valuers, take note.)
- Are our products or services appropriately priced?
- Under what circumstances are we able to increase our prices?
- Do our margins enable us to provide the appropriate levels of service and support to our customers?
- Are our margins satisfactory to enable us to meet our costs and profit targets?
- If not, what can we do about it? Can we renegotiate with our suppliers? Should we look to change suppliers? Should we seek to change the product mix?
- Do our salespeople understand our products well enough?
- How long since we talked to our main customers and asked whether our products or services are meeting their requirements?
- Do we ensure that customer feedback is communicated to the product development people?
- Are there additional products or services that we can easily offer to our existing clients?
- Do we have the right distribution channels?
- If we covered a larger geographical area, are there existing clients who would benefit from that, and would those clients help to fund our geographical expansion?
- In what way is our product or service better than that of our competitors?
- When compared to our competitors, do we have product disadvantages?

When did I last **phone reception** from **outside the company** and **experience** how our **customers** are **greeted?**

- How can we overcome that disadvantage?
- Whose job is it to lead that challenge?
- What are the things that we do better than our competitors?
- What are the things that our competitors do better than us?
- Where is the competitor that we can't see and what are we doing to take our business/industry to a different level?
- What can we do to make things difficult for our competitors?
- Do our competitors have clients that we should be targeting?
- Do our competitors have people that we should be targeting?

Sales and marketing

- What do we look like to the outside observer?
- What do people see when they look at our company, our facilities, our people, our marketing material, our website, etc.? (First impressions count.)
- How do we answer our phones?
- How long since I phoned reception from outside the company and experienced the way customers are greeted?
- How long since I listened to my own voicemail message. How does it sound to a customer?
- When I leave messages for others, how much thought do I give to what I say?
- What is our market position?
- Are we low cost or high value?
- Does our customer base reflect a positioning that is different from what we think?
- Who is the ideal customer that we are targeting?
- Is our advertising cost effective?
- Is our advertising fresh in the eyes of the customer?
- Does our marketing activity accurately reflect what we are trying to achieve for our customers?
- Does our marketing activity accurately target the clients we are pursuing?
- Do I know where 50% of next year's revenue is coming from?
- Are our goals and targets achievable in the current market?
- What is my total revenue target for the next 12 months?
- How much of that revenue will come from new clients?
- How many new clients do we need to approach, with our average conversion rates, to meet that new business target?
- Who is responsible for maintaining existing clients?
- Who is responsible for targeting new business?

Do we have enough **leaders?**

- Were our sales teams involved or consulted in helping to set the budgets? (It sounds obvious, I know, but it doesn't often happen.)
- How many clients, based on current spend, do we need to enable us to achieve our revenue budgets?
- Do we have enough salespeople to cover that number of clients?
- Do we have enough clients, current and targeted, to meet those revenue targets?
- How do we manage our stock to enable us to ensure we can supply sufficient product to enable us to hit our revenue targets? (Again, it sounds obvious, but I have seen plenty of businesses selling to target but failing to supply.)
- Do our salespeople understand our clients' businesses well enough?
- Are our salespeople accountable for their performance within a measureable market (i.e. a product category, a geographical area, a group of customers, or a channel)?
- How often do we conduct performance reviews with the salespeople?
- Do we ensure that customer feedback is communicated to the sales and product development people?
- Are our salespeople appropriately presented at all times?
- Are our salespeople encouraged to give accurate customer feedback to management?
- Do our sales leaders and managers spend enough time with our customers?

People

- Do our people know what we are trying to achieve?
- Do our people know what they are meant to do?
- Do our people know whether we are on track or behind plan?
- How long is it since I walked the floor and talked to our people, without a particular agenda?
- How often should we aim to have a big room meeting with all of our people?
- Do we have the right people?
- Do we have enough leaders?
- Are our people good enough?
- What are the areas of our business where our people are really strong?
- In what areas of the business do I believe that we have people weaknesses?
- Do the competition have better people?
- If so, who can we steal?
- Do we have a pipeline of talent that we are currently working on recruiting?
- Who would we like to target?

When did I last have a **constructive one on one discussion**, with one of the **lowest paid** people in my team?

- How long since we talked to those people who are struggling?
- How can we help them?
- What skills are we lacking?
- Where are the innovative recruitment solutions? Where should we be looking for better people or tomorrow's people?
- How often do we conduct performance reviews?
- How many times do we interview people for the six most critical roles in our business?
- Is that enough?
- Are we effective at letting poor performers go in a respectful and professional manner?
- Do we have a drug and alcohol policy and do we abide by it?
- Does every member of our team have a current job description?
- Does every member of our team have a component of his or her remuneration that is a form of bonus?
- Does that bonus align with the core objectives of the company?
- Do our remuneration structures align with or reflect the core objectives of the company, across all roles?
- When was the last time we celebrated a success of the company with our people?
- When was the last time we publicly celebrated the individual success of one of our people?
- When was the last time I had a proper and constructive one-on-one conversation with one of the lowest-paid people in my team?
- How long has it been since we reviewed our induction process for new people?
- Do we give them sufficient information during the induction process?
- What is day one like for our new people?
- Can we make it better?
- When was the last time I took a new person out for lunch on their first day?
- Do we give our people permission to help us be successful?
- When our people leave, irrespective of the reasons, do we treat them with respect?
- What can we do for our people on their birthday that's a bit different?
- Do we make it easy for new mothers to return to work after their baby is born?
- Do we create opportunities for those same new mums to catch up on their career, if they want to?
- What is the spread of gender across the business?
- Are we delivering to our goals around equal opportunity and remuneration?
- Thinking about everything that has to be done within the business, are we clear

What does our most **demanding customer** expect? Could we do that for **everyone?**

on who is responsible in every case? (Nothing happens unless it's someone's job.)

- Do our personnel engagement strategies, including remuneration and allocation of responsibility, reflect the overall objectives of the company?
- Our community now includes Asian, Indian and people of Middle Eastern decent to a far greater degree than ever before. How inclusive are we of these groups, in terms of respecting their qualifications, hiring them and engaging them when they get here?
- Are we a good employer?
- What is it like to work for us?
- Do we meet the expectations of people when they join?
- What is our personnel turnover rate and how does that compare to our industry?
- Do our people, who are closer to the customer than I am, see us doing stupid things?
- How do I find out what those things are and what we can do about them?
- Do we create the opportunity for our people to come to us with ideas for improvement in a way that is not threatening?

Customers

- What is so hard about providing great customer service?
- Do I know my top 10 most important customers?
- How well do we know the top 20% of our customers?
- Have I spoken directly to a customer today?
- How do we describe our typical client?
- What types of new clients do we want?
- What is the average client spend when they interact with our company?
- How can we grow their average spend?
- What is the ideal-sized client in revenue terms?
- Do we understand what our customer is trying to achieve when they buy goods or services from us?
- Do our clients have requirements that we are currently unable to satisfy?
- Would it be possible for us to expand our activity in order to satisfy those requirements?
- How would we go about that?
- How quickly do we respond to client orders, queries, complaints and requests for information?
- Are those timelines satisfactory?
- If not, what is the impact of our underperformance in this area?

What do our **customers think of us**?

- How do those timelines compare with our customer expectations?
- Can we do better?
- Whose job is it to improve our customer service performance?
- What does our most demanding customer expect?
- Do we deliver to that client's expectations?
- What would it take to deliver to all of our clients at that standard?
- What do our customers think of us?
- What do we want our customers to think of us?
- Do we talk to our customers in their language or ours? (Car dealers, computer salespeople and finance industry execs, take note.)
- Are we conscious that we do what we do every day, but for our customers, they work with people like us only occasionally?
- Do we treat their enquiry with the respect and importance that they would expect?
- Are we trying different things?

We often **complain** about what **Generation F expect**. But there is nothing **unique** about **their requirements**. **Gen F** are **simply asking** for the **things** we should be **doing** for **all of our people**. It's just that previous generations **didn't have the nerve** to **demand** the **information** or the **attention**.

Sample questions for conducting a job interview

I've seen plenty of people run out of conversation a short way into the traditional interview process. So I have outlined below some questions to use when you are interviewing people. Some of the questions will apply to someone applying for an individual role, while others reflect people applying for management or leadership roles. You don't need to use all of the questions, and, of course, some of them overlap. However, there are enough ideas here to ensure that your interviews are constructive sessions that help you to get the best outcomes.

1. How did you find out about this role becoming available?
2. What was it about the role that made you decide to apply?
3. Of course, I have your CV in front of me, but can you tell me about your background in your own words?
4. Can you please tell me what you know about this role?
5. How do you think your background would assist you in being successful in the role?
6. What are the specific skills that you feel you will bring to it?
7. If you could do the things you would like to do in this role, what do you think could be achieved?
8. Have you taken on something similar before?
9. If so, can you tell us a bit about that?
10. What experience do you have in leading or managing a team?
11. Can you please tell me about your approach to leading a team of people?
12. What are the key things that you feel are important in managing teams?
13. What are your preferred ways of communicating with your team?
14. If you are successful in being appointed to the role, do you have a view on what you will be trying to achieve?
15. If you were looking back in a couple of years, what would success in this role look like from your perspective?
16. How well do you get on with other people?
17. Are there certain people you get on with better than others?
18. What are the key factors in building high-performing teams?
19. Can you give me an example of where you have developed and maintained the high performance of a team?
20. Can you give me an example of a difficult person you have had to manage and what you did with them?

The most important thing
in communication
is to hear what isn't being said.

Peter Drucker (1909–2005)
Bestselling author
and management expert

21. What about a high performer who was getting a bit too big for his or her boots?
22. How would you regard your relationships with your clients/customers in your current role?
23. Are there any client relationships that were at risk of going bad that you have had to recover?
24. Can you give us an example of what you did about that?
25. Can you please tell me about a project that you led that went really well?
26. What was the key to the success?
27. Can you please tell me about a project that you led that didn't go well?
28. What was the key to the failure?
29. What were the key differences between those two outcomes and what are the lessons for you as a manager?
30. Most people in management roles have a real mix of factors to balance. How do you go about balancing the various issues and opportunities around you?
31. Can you give us an example of a major change within a business that you have been involved in?
32. How did the changes affect you?
33. Were you required to take a leadership role in that programme?
34. How did it go?
35. In your management career, has there been a time when you have had to let people go or reduce the size of your team?
36. How do you feel about that sort of thing?
37. What are you really good at?
38. What are the areas, if any, where you find yourself struggling, or areas where you don't feel strong enough?
39. If you could, what is an area of your skill set that you would like to improve?
40. Tell me about your best recruit.
41. Have you ever had a new recruit that didn't work out?
42. Where do you think it went wrong and what did you learn from that experience?
43. Have you ever had a time when the job has gotten on top of you?
44. How did you manage to get back on top?
45. Did you seek outside help or input or did you just work through it yourself?
46. Are you good at recognising when you need to ask for help?
47. Can you recall an idea you have come up with that was regarded as highly creative or innovative?
48. What do you love about your current position?
49. How has your current role changed since you started it?

The way to **get started**
is to **quit talking**
and **start doing**.

Walt Disney
Disneyland

50. What makes you feel that it might be time to move on from your current role?
51. Can you tell me about something you have done in your previous role that you are particularly proud of?
52. What about outside of work — something that you have done that you are really proud of?
53. What do you do when you are not working — what outside interests do you have?
54. If you could do any job in the world, what would it be and why?
55. If you could be the boss/Prime Minister/President of the USA/head of the United Nations (choose one) for one day, what would you do to change things?

Average organisations
will always **lose**
above-average people.

Sample questions for the person being interviewed

Usually, as part of the interview process, I always like to give candidates the opportunity to ask any questions they might have. Frequently, I am surprised when the questions don't come, or the candidate runs out of questions after one or two attempts. It's a bit difficult to draft a list of questions without a specific role in mind, but here are some generic ones to consider applying to a role you are interviewing for.

1. Can you please describe the three or four key objectives that the company is trying to achieve?
2. How would this proposed role (or my proposed department) contribute to the achievement of those objectives?
3. What is the company's staff turnover rate?
4. If high: Why do you think that is so high?
5. If high: Do you have any initiatives or projects that are currently under way to try to reduce that?
6. If low: That's very good for this industry; what do you think have been the key ingredients to keeping it that low?
7. What do our customers think of us?
8. As I understand it, this is an existing role. What were the reasons for the departure of the person who previously occupied this role? (Note: They may have been promoted, left to join another organisation, or terminated — it is helpful for you to know this in terms of what you may be walking into.) OR
9. As I understand it, this is a new role. What has prompted the creation of this new role/new department?
10. How would you describe the performance of the current team that I will be leading?
11. How does that performance compare with the expectations of management in respect of that area of the business?
12. Other than changing the leader, what other initiatives have been tried or are being considered to turn things around?

Epilogue

I wish for you a career that is filled with wonderful experiences and positive outcomes.

Remember that business is supposed to be challenging and difficult and frustrating.

But you will also experience accomplishment, fulfilment and reward.

You will have days when you win and days when you lose.

But you have the opportunity to be the best you can be,

so why not try?

Try to do things that others won't do.

Look for things that you are passionate about, and try to make a difference.

Don't be afraid to break the mould.

Don't be afraid to try a different way.

Well-intentioned failure is okay, as long as you don't give up.

There may be bad experiences, but there's no such thing as bad experience.

And the best advice that I can give is that you seek out experiences,

rather than salaries, bonuses or job titles.

Keep growing, keep learning, keep asking questions and helping others.

Remember, leadership is an important responsibility, and leaders change the lives of the people they work with.

So look after yourself and your family.

Be the best you can be.

And have fun.

Thanks for reading.

And good luck with your leadership journey.

I wish you every success.

Keep in touch.

sayhello@brucecotterill.com
www.brucecotterill.com
Twitter: @brucecotterill1

Acknowledgements

As noted by the credit at the beginning of this book, my parents were the source of my desire to be the best that I could. They were always encouraging, and although they didn't know it at the time, their hard work — at times with both of them working two jobs — and determination to succeed bred in me a desire for a successful life.

My career is a function of a few people who have had a wonderful influence on me. As mentioned earlier, Douglas Hitchcock was an outstanding mentor and motivator who believed in giving young people an opportunity, often before we were ready. There are a great many of us who have much to thank him for. I have Doug to thank for Monday morning meetings, the sales pipeline, and being 'at the line', that most important of time management disciplines. My only wish of Doug is that he would write his book. It would be far more interesting than most.

Roger Cook was the CEO of Colliers Jardine and he came into my life at a time when I was looking to take a step up and lead a substantial business. Roger is a wonderful leader who taught me much, including the question that I continue to use to this day: 'What would you do if you owned the business?' We shared many challenging times, and late-night conversations, as we fought for our business. The market-leading status of Colliers International (as it is now called) today, across Asia-Pacific and globally, is in large part a result of his unselfish and total commitment to the company throughout the 1990s. During the difficult early days at Colliers in Australia, Robert McCuaig, Paul Ward and Bill McHarg, all legends of the Australian real estate industry in their own right, were supportive beyond measure. As a young Kiwi in the Australian property business, I will never forget their help.

John Alexander is a uniquely capable executive. As CEO of PBL Media, he led both Channel 9 and Australian Consolidated Press through the turbulence that was the media industry at the turn of the century. We arrived at the company just two months apart, and his clarity of thought and leadership were compelling. John has had his critics, many of whom are derived from those difficult times. However, from my perspective I have nothing but positive things to say about his leadership and his support for his executive team. He gave me what I wanted most — the time and space to turn the business around and get the best results that we possibly could. John remains, unquestionably, the most intelligent person I have ever worked with, and my memories of our time together are full of lessons about publishing, television, leadership and, of course, quarterly reviews.

Graeme Evans, a long-time grocer and retailer, was my chairman at Canterbury

International. Again, the days were difficult, extremely so at times, and yet his steadfast support, the kind that only comes with many years' experience, gave me the comfort that I was on the right track. Difficult decisions are always easier when those whom you respect are supportive of your actions.

Alongside these wonderful mentors I feel privileged to have been given wonderful opportunities by, and enjoyed wise counsel and amazing input from, a wide range of people including Christopher Bielenberg in London, the late Kerry Packer from Australia, New Zealander Professor David Teece at Berkeley University in California, publisher Barry Colman, the late John Waller of PWC, and Yellow Pages industry veteran, Jim Smith from Colorado. All of these people shaped the things we did and the decisions we made. Many of our conversations will be long forgotten by them, but I remember them fondly.

A CEO can't function without an assistant and I have been fortunate to have three who were outstanding. To Adrienne Buttner, Kiri Leonard and Heather McGregor, thank you for running my life when I needed all the help I could get.

A year ago I ran into a former colleague from my days as Chairman of the New Zealand Magazine Publishers Association. Reg Birchfield was a founder of New Zealand's *National Business Review* (*NBR*) and a business publisher without peer. When he asked me what I was up to, I made the mistake of telling him that I was in the process of writing a book. From that moment onwards, he has been a source of inspiration and drive that has seen me complete this manuscript far more quickly, and hopefully far more professionally, than I might otherwise have. Reg, I hope that you are as happy with the result as I am.

Martin Taylor and I have had our paths connect a number of times to date. We both worked in the computer industry in the 1980's, and met up again when we were both in the magazine industry, in his case as Managing Director of publisher IDG Communications. Martin is now in the book publishing business through his company Digital Strategies, and he has been responsible for guiding me through the process of getting this work completed and published. Two members of Martin's team have delivered wonderful work on my behalf. Eva Chan had the task of proofreading and correcting the manuscript. And book designer Nick Turzynski was given the job of managing the variables around left hand pages and right hand pages that each required different design treatment. As you have seen, despite the challenges, he made it work and the reader friendly text is a reflection of his efforts.

A leader is only as good as the team he works with, and I have been fortunate to work with some outstanding people. To the teams at Office Automation Company, Realty Brokers, REL Consulting, Colliers, ACP, Canterbury, Gresham Private

Equity, Noel Leeming, Yellow Pages, MOVE Logistics and TDDA, and the not for-profits such as Swimming New Zealand, Pinehurst School, Surf Life Saving NZ and many more, thank you for having me at your place of work and for teaching me so much in what have often been challenging circumstances.

To you, the people who read books like these, and who listen intently to the presentations from people like me in conferences around the world, thank you for your continued interest in leadership and management and in making our work environments better places. Please keep asking your questions.

* * *

Finally, during the last few months I have broken many of my own rules around work-life balance. There are three very important people in my life who have borne the brunt of my late nights and numerous weekends labouring over the words that have gone before these.

My amazing wife, Rose, has always been totally accepting of the career that I have chosen, the dinners I had to attend and the trips I have had to make. When it came to relocating countries, she was always up for the opportunity and was packing the house before I had signed the paperwork. She has also borne the lion's share of running a household with a couple of very active and busy kids.

Suzie and Fraser are the two coolest people I know, and alongside Rose, their collective support and understanding over the course of my career has allowed me to pursue some wonderful experiences and in doing so to learn many valuable lessons about life and business. As educated millennials in the new world, you both have amazing opportunities before you, and I encourage each of you to live your dreams, and make a difference to the things that you care about.

You are all amazing, successful people in your own right, and I am incredibly proud to call the three of you my family.

* * *

Lightning Source UK Ltd.
Milton Keynes UK
UKHW051121071218
333595UK00020B/258/P